The Old Days

Boscastle has a long and vibrant history of trade and occupation dating back to the Iron Age.

The Cornish Language

Boscastle's earliest settlers were Britons who spoke the Celtic tongue of Brythonic, from which the Cornish, Welsh and Breton languages evolved. Cornish (Kernewek) was once spoken throughout Cornwall until its sad demise in the 19th century. During the 20th century, a revival of interest in Cornish took place and today there are a growing number of dedicated speakers.

Early Settlers

There are more than 30 examples of Iron Age cliff castles similar to that at Willapark to be found along the coast of Cornwall.

On the headland of Willapark, some 2500 years ago, a ditch and rampart was thrown up across the neck of the headland securing a defensive settlement.

Little is known about these very early inhabitants, but archeological evidence from similar cliff castles in Cornwall reveals that they farmed the land.

350 BC - 50 AD ...

Iron Age - Willapark cliff castle is built.

480 ...

St Materiana founds a cell at Minster.

1066 ...

Norman Invasion.

1080 ...

Building of Bottreaux Castle begins.

1235 ...

The first Wellington mill is built.

1306 ...

Boscastle records 101 tax payers.

1348 ...

The Black Death - Treworld is deserted.

1377 ...

Population of Boscastle, 181.

1386 ...

Minster Priory lies in ruins.

Markets

After the Norman Conquest all the land around Boscastle was owned by the powerful Bottreaux family (originally from Anjou in France) and each farmstead had to pay a fee to till the soil.

In 1204 the Bottreaux were granted the right to hold a market here. In 1312 Edward II renewed the charter adding a licence for an annual fair on the Feast of St James the Apostle.

Later two yearly fairs were held, Lamb Fair in July and Martin's Fair in November. Credits and bills were settled at these events and great celebration dinners were given.

The weekly markets continued to be held here until 1968.

Fairs and markets brought much trade to the village, boosting the income of grocery shops, pubs, butchers, cobblers, carpenters and other businesses.

Farming

The local economy around Boscastle has always been dependent on agriculture and a rare remnant of Medieval farming practices can still be found on Forrabury Common. The Stitches (right, after harvest) are thin strips of hedgeless fields still farmed as of old. Crops are cultivated from Lady Day to Michaelmas and outside these dates the land becomes common grazing ground.

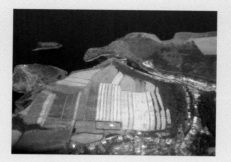

Twin Town

For much of its history Boscastle has been known as two settlements.

Top Town (right c. 1900) was up the hill and contained many businesses, including a forge, cobbler, butcher, chemist, draper and hotel, along with grocery stores, inns and carpenter shops.

Down by the harbour was Quaytown more recently known as Bridge (right c. 1890). This was the life-line for the village as road transport was poor and the only reliable means of importing and exporting goods was by sea.

1407 ...
Minster Priory ceases to exist - first rector of Minster Church appointed.

1462 ...
William de Bottreaux, the last of the family, dies at the battle of St Albans.

1584 ...
Boscastle pier is repaired by Sir Richard Grenville.

1644 ...
The English Civil War comes to Cornwall.

1740 ...
Boscastle harbour repaired.

1793 - 1815 ...
Napoleonic Wars - press gangs raid Boscastle.

1814 ...
Mansion House (Castle) demolished.

1820 ...
200 tons of manganese shipped from Boscastle.

1820 ...
Outer pier built.

1824 ...
Turner visits Boscastle - paints dramatic scenes of Willapark.

1830 ...
1000 tons of manganese shipped from Boscastle.

1836 ...
Penally House built by local merchant William Sloggatt.

1837 ...
Wesleyan Chapel built in Dunn Street - also known as Jabez Brown's Chapel.

1843 ...

Great Gale of 27th January - Forrabury Church roof blown off.

1845 ...

26th Jul -, fatal accident at Wheal Neptune Mine. Wheal Boscastle operational.

1850 ...

Height of the port's trade - 300 ships per year.

1852 ...

Boscastle Hotel renamed Scott's Wellington Hotel after the Iron Duke's death.

1868 ...

Forrabury Church restored. Minster's roof collapses.

1870 ...

Thomas Hardy comes to restore St Juliot's church.

1886 ...

New Road is built.

1893 ...

The railway comes to Camelford.

1941 ...

Sea mine explodes against the outer harbour wall causing irreparable damage.

1946 ...

Most of the village of Boscastle sold as part of an estate for £90,000.

1955 ...

The National Trust begins to acquire land at Boscastle, when T. P. Fulford gives it the harbour and 61 acres.

1957 ...

The Great Flood - the old bridge is swept away.

Trade & Industry

The 1841 Boscastle census shows a thriving community of 360 people including tailors, milliners, cordwainers, wool-combers, maltsters, bakers, merchants, carriers, grocers, innkeepers, ironmongers, butchers, cobblers, millers, carpenters, blacksmiths, quarrymen, masons, farmers, sailors and fishermen. There was also a customs officer, doctor, chemist, solicitor, post master, harbour master, accountant, schoolmaster and a surveyor.

The photographs below dating from the 1870s show many of the mercantile warehouses, offices, stables and workshops of the Quaytown traders. The numbered points opposite list the former use of some of the village's buildings, many of which are still recognisable today.

(1) **The building housing Boscastle's new Visitor Centre.** This has had numerous past uses including being a fish cellar, village hall, carpenter's shop, the Apollo Cinema and a restaurant.

(2) National Trust shop. **Formerly named Bottreaux Court, this was once a fish cellar and manure store.**

(3) Witchcraft Museum. **Formerly a smoke-house and store.**

(4) Harbour Lights. **Totally rebuilt after it was washed away in the floods of 2004; the original structure was once a pig sty.**

(5) Harbour Terrace (now private houses). **Formerly a salt store and warehouse called Fox's Cellars, with adjoining smoke-house.**

(6) Seagulls (cottage and shop). **Formerly a manganese mill, then a carpenter and wheelwright's workshop.**

(7) Valency Row (now private houses). **Once included two inns, The Robin and The Ship, a malt house and Valency House, the home of Thomas Avery.**

(8) The Car Park. **Formerly lawns and gardens belonging to the Manor House.**

(9) Cobweb Inn. **Until 1947, this was an off-licence, warehouse and general store.**

(10) The Old Manor House (restaurant). **Once the Manor offices.**

(11) Courtyard frontage of Bridge Walk shops. **Once the site of Ward's general storehouse, demolished in the 1970s when the road was widened.**

(12) Bridge House. **Previously a grocery and general goods shop.**

(13) The Riverside Hotel. **This was built around 1584 by Sir Richard Grenville of the "Revenge" fame.**

(14) Gallery & Rocky Road. **Once a coal store and Boscastle's first petrol station.**

(15) Otherworld. **These were once millers dwellings known as Island Cottages.**

(16) Old Mill shops. **Formerly the Wellington Old Mill - the water-wheel here, fed by a leat from the Jordan River, once provided power to grind corn and later generated electricity for the hotel.**

1962 ...

Outer pier is rebuilt by the National Trust, using stone from the old Laira Bridge, Plymouth.

1963 ...

End of the sheep fairs dating from 1204.

1994 ...

Boscastle's first Visitor Centre is built.

2004 ...

The TV series "A Seaside Parish" is premiered. The 20 episodes, document the work of Church of England clergy in Boscastle.

2004 ...

Boscastle's Visitor Centre refurbished.

2004 ...

Boscastle's flood devastates the village and demolishes the Visitor Centre and three other properties.

2005 ...

Start of Boscastle's regeneration and the Environment Agency's £4.6 million flood defence scheme, scheduled to finish by March 2008.

2006 ...

New Visitor Centre relocated and opened.

Architecture & Morality

Behind the facade of many of Boscastle's older buildings lies a hidden history of colourful past lives and traditions which have long since vanished.

Smuggling

Smuggling was a serious business along this coast during the 18th and 19th centuries. With poverty rife and extortionate taxes imposed on tea, liquor, tobacco and even salt, "free trading" became an important livelihood for many in the community.

To stem this trafficking, Revenue Men were employed and Preventative Stations set up along the coast.

Here at Boscastle a post was established to police the area between Padstow and Bude. Enforcing these Custom and Excise duties was not only an unpopular profession but also a dangerous and violent one with armed conflicts not uncommon.

The path carved into the hill above the Cobweb Inn is known as **The Private Road** and also the **Green Cut**. It was originally a private track leading from the harbour to Penally House where there were tales of smuggling and subterranean tunnels. Contraband is said to have been transported via this path to warehouses below where it was added to legitimate stocks.

Tiny windows, or **squints**, found in some of the older cottages are thought to have doubled as lookouts to warn of approaching Revenue Men.

Wrecking

Thomas Rickard Avery who lived in Valency Row was a tough merchantman and shipowner who acquired a dubious reputation amongst his contemporaries. Two accounts describe him as... *"a notorious wrecker and receiver of contraband goods"* and *"a violent and wicked man"*.

It was said that as soon as any ship was spotted in distress Avery would not let her out of his sight until she came aground; then he would claim the salvage rights and make an enormous profit.

In 1829 a case was brought against Thomas Avery citing that a large quantity of hops had found their way into his hands. The vessel, carrying the cargo to Ireland, was wrecked near Bude in suspicious circumstances and the Coastguard were promptly dispatched to protect it from looters. Avery consequently arrived to claim the cargo with an authority from the ship's Master, but this was refused. Avery then attacked the Preventative Men, who defended themselves with their swords.

The following morning, as the Guards were escorting the goods to Bude, they were once again set upon by Avery's mob who this time successfully seized the shipment.

Avery was later found guilty of the offence and was forced to pay costs and damages of over £1000.

Phantom Lights

On the eve of December 16th 1858, local sailors and Boscastle businessman Jabez Brown saw a mysterious fiery cloud sailing up the valley, gliding over Thomas Avery's house and onwards towards Minster church where Avery's family were buried.

At 5am the next morning, as a storm raged, Avery was heard pacing about in his room. An hour later a large wave entered the harbour, washing away one of his vessels. A servant on hearing the news called on his master only to find him dead.

Avery was buried on Christmas Day, aged 74, amid terrible storms of thunder, hail and wind which roused many of the local people.

The distinctive **whitewashed tower** on the summit of Willapark is thought to date from the 1820s and was built as a pleasure house by the local merchant, and some say smuggler, Thomas Avery. Ironically the building later served as a Coastguard lookout and was recently re-established for this purpose.

Liquor

In 1830 tax duty on beer and cider was removed and with the payment of two guineas a year a licence could be obtained to retail these commodities. By the mid 18th century Boscastle boasted a staggering 20 ale pubs, "kiddlywinks" and brew-houses.

Establishments such as the Old Boscastle Inn, half way down Fore Street, the Brig Inn, situated at the top of the village and the Ship Inn, in Valency Row near the harbour, have long since been converted into dwellings, but the Wellington and the Napoleon remain.

The **Old Boscastle Inn**, dating back to the 1700s, brewed its own beer and was a known smuggler's depot. It ceased trading in the early 1900s.

The Wellington Hotel
Dating from the 1600s, this is one of the oldest coaching inns in north Cornwall and was an important stage for the Exeter to Falmouth mail coaches until the 1920s.

Originally called the Bos Castle Hotel, it was renamed on the death of the Iron Duke in 1852 and was largely rebuilt in 1860 to its present day form featuring the striking castellated turret.

A number of prominent persons have stayed here including Thomas Hardy, Edward VII with a "lady friend", and actor Sir Henry Irving.

The **River Jordan** flows underneath the Wellington Hotel, pictured here prior to its castellated conversion in the 1860s.

The Napoleon Inn
Situated at the top of the village, is this attractive 16th century inn. According to one Boscastle tradition the inn was used as a recruiting office during the Napoleonic Wars and the landlord himself joined Wellington's ranks and fought at Waterloo. On returning home he was nicknamed the "Napoleon man" and consequently christened the inn accordingly. Another tale states that it was so named because it was actually a place used to recruit volunteers for the enemy!

A more plausible clue to the **Napoleon Inn's** name comes from a report dated 1859, when its landlord William Bone (Bone / Bonaparte) was fined for keeping a disorderly house and allowing gambling. Boney's Bar is still found in the pub.

The Cobweb Inn

Dating from the 1700s, this did not acquire a full licence as a pub until 1947. Prior to this it had been an off licence and warehouse known as the Launceston Cellar. Beer, wine and spirits were bottled and stored here supplying inns and pubs of

Once the inn's bar was festooned with **cobwebs**, a legacy from the storehouse days when it was thought that spiders would help to keep flies away from the stored goods.

the area. Corn was kept on its top floor and manure on the third!!

Redemption

During the Napoleonic Wars a fully laden vessel, owned by wealthy wine and spirit merchants from Boscastle, encountered a French privateer who gave chase.

The Cornish captain headed for Boscastle harbour, with its hidden entrance, and thus evaded capture by the French. In gratitude for this narrow escape the two merchants, Messrs. Sloggatt & Rosevear, donated money to fund the building of a teetotal Methodist Chapel!

Despite the number of public houses in Boscastle in the 19th century, like the rest of Cornwall, it was a stronghold of Methodism. The village boasted three different chapels with another two nearby at Trevalga and Treworld.

Of the many active chapels once to be found in the area only one survives today, the **United Methodist Church** in Fore Street, which was opened in 1825.

1821...
Murder committed at the **Garland Inn**.

1857...
16th January - riot at the **Brig Inn**.

1860...
Landlord of the **Napoleon Inn** fined for being drunk and incapable and for threatening the police.

1877...
Mr Forward of **The Ship**, charged with the adulteration of beer with salt to promote thirst - fined £1.

A New Harvest

During the 19th century Boscastle experienced a great change in direction, transforming it from a busy working port to a holiday destination within a few decades.

Victorian Visitors

In the mid 19th century, Boscastle's inhabitants began to experience a new harvest. The area's associations with the Arthurian legends and the beauty of its dramatic coastline attracted poets, artists and Victorian gentlemen of leisure. The village became a key destination on the itinerary of the West Country grand tour, drawing notable visitors such as...

J. M. W. Turner (1775-1851)

Turner is perhaps Britain's most famous painter. He was enormously prolific, producing some 550 oil paintings, over 2,000 finished watercolours and some 30,000 works on paper.

He toured Cornwall many times, the first visit being in 1811. Turner came to Boscastle on one of his numerous sketching trips as he was particularly interested in the area's Arthurian connection.

Turner's watercolour of Boscastle harbour c.1824, now housed in the Ashmolean Museum, Oxford, is executed in his typically dramatic and romantic style.

Sir Henry Irving (1838-1905)

Irving, whose original name was John Brodribb, became the first actor ever to be knighted. He was brought up in Cornwall and was a frequent visitor to Boscastle during the latter part of the 19th century. Here, it is said, he was interested in the reputed magical powers of a Boscastle woman to whom he gave a regular allowance in return for her psychic advice.

Sir Henry Irving's reputation for originality, stage presence and the brilliancy of his productions brought him international fame. But in 1897 his fortunes changed and in 1905, after a series of disasters, Irving died penniless at the age of 68.

Alfred Lord Tennyson (1809-1892)

Tennyson is often regarded as the greatest poet of the Victorian age. In 1850, he was created Poet Laureate, a position he held for 42 years. In 1848 Tennyson toured North Cornwall to conduct research and although Tintagel's haunting ruins provided his main inspiration, he was also known to have visited Boscastle.

One of **Tennyson's** most famous works is "Idylls of the King" (1885), a series of narrative poems based on the Arthurian legends.

Rev. R. S. Hawker (1804-1875)

Poet, author and vicar of Morwenstow, Hawker was a regular visitor to Boscastle where his brother Claude lived at Penally House. Hawker, like many of his Victorian contemporaries, was caught up in the obsession with the Arthurian sagas. He produced a long series of romantic and religious poems which gained notice from figures like Dickens and Tennyson, who visited him in 1848.

One of **Hawker's** finest works, the "Quest of the San Graal" published in 1864, is an epic poem based on the legend of the Holy Grail.

Locomotion

The coming of the railway, first to Launceston in 1886 and then to Camelford in 1893, had fundamental implications for Boscastle.

Two companies, the Great Western Railway and the Southern Railway, developed routes to the West Country making travel increasingly available to a wider section of the public.

The advent of motorcars and organised coach tours further increased the numbers of visitors to the village.

Touring the remote villages of north Cornwall was no longer the reserve of the privileged classes - 20th century tourism had arrived.

On alighting at Camelford Station passengers for Boscastle would take the horse-drawn carriage on to the staging post at the **Wellington Hotel**. The village continued to be dependent on this mode of transport until the 1920s. With the coming of the motor car a local family changed the old coal store near the bridge into a garage where vehicles could be hired and serviced.

Prince Bira, a member of Siam's royal family and grandson of King Mongkut of "The King and I" fame, stored his racing motorcar Romulus here during the 1940s.

THE PORT

Road transport until the 18th century was almost impossible in Cornwall. The only way to bring regular supplies into a coastal village like Boscastle and to export produce was by ship, making any port a very valuable asset.

Early Trade

Evidence from excavations on Tintagel Island show that trade was taking place hereabouts with Mediterranean merchants during the Dark Ages. When William de Bottreaux arrived in the 12th century he would have relied almost totally on ships to supply his castle.

Research shows that a quay in the harbour was twice rebuilt in the early part of Queen Elizabeth I's reign and cost the the inhabitants over £200.

In 1584 at a cost of £100, a new quay was built in a different location by the Lord Lieutenant of Cornwall, Sir Richard Grenville, who was later to perish on board the Revenge. The harbour walls were built with the slates placed vertically with no mortar to bind them, and apart from some additions and repairs in 1740, they have remained intact ever since.

A second harbour wall was built in 1820 as a breakwater to help curb the devastating swells that entered the harbour. During World War II a sea-mine exploded nearby damaging the pier and by 1942 the sea had demolished it entirely. The present day pier was built in 1962 by the National Trust using stone salvaged from Plymouth's old Laira Bridge.

" [Richard Grenville of Cornwall] brought to England twenty two Spaniards whom he treated as slaves, making them carry stones on their backs all day for some building operations of his and chaining them up all night. Twenty of them have died or escaped..."

Extract from a contemporary letter, 1584.

"He would carouse three or four glasses of wine, and in a bravery take the glasses between his teeth and crash them in pieces and swallow them down, so that oftentimes the blood ran out of his mouth without any harm at all unto him."

A description of **Sir Richard Grenville's** behaviour while dining with Spanish captains.

Boscastle c.1940 with the original **outer harbour wall**. The inner harbour pier has an anti-submarine extension at its end.

Shipping

The mid-nineteenth century was the heyday of trading activity in the harbour area of Boscastle known as Quaytown. As many as 300 vessels a year visited the port despite its tricky, dog-leg entrance which limited its use.

Hobbling

The **Hobbling boat** was Boscastle's version of the Cornish Pilot Gig which was originally rowed out to guide incoming vessels. In most other harbours this was a fiercely competitive task, as to get their pilot on board first meant getting the job and hence the payment.

Navigating sailing ships in and out of the port was a tricky business. In foul weather it could be extremely dangerous, if not impossible.

The solution was the 30 foot hobbling boat with a crew of nine which would be rowed out to ships anchored off-shore and used to tow them safely into the harbour.

Leaving port was even more complicated. Teams of men stationed on both sides of the entrance would haul on lines, positioned by the hobblers, to guide the outgoing vessel.

Gig Racing

Today pilot gigs are raced for sport, with around 100 clubs across the globe. Most are based in Cornwall, Devon and the Isles of Scilly, which host the World Pilot Gig Championships each May.

All modern racing gigs have to conform to the exact specification of the Treffry, built in 1838 by William Peters of St. Mawes and still raced by the Newquay Gig Club.

Boscastle's first gig, the aptly named **Torrent**, was made by Peter Williams at Bodinnick (right: under construction) and launched in 2006. It was partly funded by donations after the Floods of 2004 and is a symbol of the community's spirit and resilience.

The two larger ships pictured in this photo, c.1890, are **Topsail Schooners** - these were the work-horses of the Cornish coast, known for their light construction, speed and sailing ability. Their strong, wide hulls enabled them to rest on the harbour floor for loading and unloading goods.

Probably the most frequent visitors to Boscastle were Ketches - beamy, two-masted vessels that could carry up to 100-tons of cargo. The Thomasine & Mary (built in 1855 and converted to ketch rig at a later date), was one of six ships built in Boscastle at the shipyard owned by merchant / landowner Thomas R. Avery.

According to local historian W.F.A. Burnard, the last ship to be built here was the Springflower, a single masted Smack that was launched on the 2nd of May 1857. She was considered by her owners to have been next to the fastest ship afloat and regularly crossed the Atlantic bringing back pitchpine timber.

Many of the harbour's open boats would have been rigged as **Luggers** - with distinctive, four sided sails. These are said to have once been favoured by smugglers as they could outrun the Revenue cutters. However, most were used for lobster and crab fishing.

The 90-ton **Francis Beddoe**, shown here leaving port in 1916, was the last cargo vessel to unload coal here. Among the other cargoes traded were slate, lime, liquor, cereals, timber, manganese and iron.

Imports & Exports

The **port** was at its busiest during the summer months as winter weather was notorious along this stretch of coast and allowed only the occasional ship into the harbour. During these hectic months as many as a dozen ships could be seen moored in the harbour with trains of horse-drawn wagons loading and unloading goods.

Boscastle's harbour c.1890

Trade from the harbour stretched over the waters to America, Ireland, France, Belgium, London, Liverpool, South Wales and Bristol.

In 1870 alone, 4000 tons of coal were imported, along with 250 tons of wine, beer and spirits, 150 tons of brick, 150 tons of groceries, 200 tons of timber, 130 tons of iron, 80 tons of tiles, 300 tons of manure and 150 tons of corn.

As for exports, 50 tons of corn, 50 tons of slate and 250 tons of China clay were shipped out from here. Other exports included bark for tanning and, for a period, manganese ore obtained from Trebursey mine near Launceston. However the port's sea trade fell into decline with the arrival of the North Cornwall Railway at Camelford in 1893.

Lime & coal

Lime is scarce in Cornwall but demand for it was high, as a soil improver and to make mortar and limewash. Great amounts of limestone were imported into the village from Swansea and was burnt in two lime kilns, one of which still stands, next door to the Visitor Centre.

There are no coal measures in the county, so this valuable fuel also had to be imported from South Wales. As much as 8000 tons were shipped into the harbour in one season. This fuel was for domestic use as well as for burning lime in the kilns.

A Watery Grave

"From Padstow Point to Lundy Light, is a watery grave by day or night"

The north coast of Cornwall has always been notoriously dangerous for shipping and had a fearful reputation among mariners in the days of sail. Over the centuries, Westerly gales and jutting reefs have wrecked hundreds of vessels and claimed many lives. The following chronology lists ships recorded lost along the 11 mile stretch of coast between Crackington Haven and Tintagel.

"It is unlucky to kill a gull - they contain the souls of sailors lost at sea."

"Never say the words drowned, church, hare, rabbit, pig or fox at sea."

"Two-decker is the taboo name for four-legged animals."

"A naked woman on board will calm the sea - hence naked figureheads."

1780
Fair Trader: V (voyage): Bristol to Boscastle. C (cargo): Unknown. W (wrecked): near Boscastle.... total loss.

1792
Thomas: V: Waterford to London. W: near Boscastle.... total loss.

1804
Sally: C: Roofing slates. W: Boscastle....
"Proving leaky, the captain was under the necessity of running her ashore at Boscastle to save the lives of his people; and it being low water, she soon went to pieces."

1807
Young Henry: W: Tintagel.... total loss.

1811
Adventure: W: Tintagel Head.... total loss.

1815
Friends Goodwill: W: Boscastle.... total loss.

1822
John & Sarah: V: Wexford to London. C: Butter. W: near Boscastle....
"On Thursday afternoon the vessel was seen off Padstow, but the tremendous ground sea prevented her from entering, and they were driven back to St. Ginnis. 300 barrels of butter, of the 1,500 taken on board, have been taken into store at Boscastle. Captain Parnall was a very deserving young man, whose body was found and taken in a hearse to Padstow, where his family reside. The body of another of the crew, called Gammin, has also been recovered."

1823
Mary Ann: W: Boscastle.... total loss.

1824
Spanish Patriot: C: Wine. W: Boscastle....
"25 hogsheads and 17 pipes of wine, some full, others only partly full, a few bags of shumack and some cork were landed from the vessel. The hull below the bands was entirely destroyed, some of the spars, rigging and sails had been saved."
Farmer: C: Slate stone. W: Tintagel.... total loss.

1825
Roger Hayes: C: Oats. W: near Boscastle.... total loss.

The **Thyra** in 1896 "... *was sighted from land at 7am flying signal of distress. Shortly before 8am the Bude lifeboat crew was summoned and launched to their rescue. On reaching the vessel her foretop mast was found to be gone, her sails and rigging a complete wreck. The crew was taken off and the lifeboat left with two small lifeboats in tow and made for Boscastle, the vessel having been abandoned...*"

1826

Narrow Escape: C: Roofing slates. W: Tintagel....

"Was wrecked last week in one of the creeks near Tintagel by the sudden rising of a ground sea which dashed her against the rocks, fortunately enabling her crew to gain the shore safely."

1827

To: V: Jersey to Cardiff C: Various. W: Tintagel.... total loss.

1828

London: V: Newport to London. C: Iron. W: Tintagel....

"Some fragments of this vessel have come on shore, the vessel having supposed foundered on the 9th inst. The crew took to their own boat and arrived at Padstow."

1829

Pendarves: V: at moorings. C: Slate stone. W: Boscastle....

"Parted her moorings this morning and went ashore, and is likely to go to pieces before the next tide. Part of her stores will be saved, but it is regretted she was not insured."

Mar Ann: W: Boscastle, Widemouth.... total loss.

1831

Emma: C: Coal. W: near Boscastle.... total loss.

1833

Sheba: W: Boscastle.... total loss.

Albion: W: near Tintagel.... total loss.

Ferret: W: Tintagel.... total loss.

1837

Hope: C: Roofing slates. W: Boscastle.... materials were saved.

Affo: W: Boscastle.... grounded.

1841

Cassandra: V: to Constantinople. C: Coal. W: Boscastle....

"On Monday a large barque passed west of here and is reported to have foundered off Boscastle. A Port Isaac boatman reports having spoken to her... seen off Boscastle about noon, apparently waterlogged, all her rudder gone, she seemed quite unmanageable and sank about 4.30pm between Boscastle and Bude, about one mile offshore. Her crew all perished having no boats..."

1842

Perseverance: C: Roofing slates. W: Trebarwith....

"Smashed up before she could get out to sea."

Canadian: V: Boscastle to France. C: Roofing slates. W: near Tintagel....

"Caught by a squall, went on shore and became a total loss during a gale the following night."

1843

Sarah: V: Neath to Teignmouth. W: Tintagel Head.... foundered.

1844

Jessie Logan: V: Calcutta to Liverpool. C: Hides; rice; dyewood. W: Boscastle....

"Whilst running for the shelter of Tintagel or Bude Haven before a strong north westerly wind, the wind increased to gale force, the ship became unmanageable, and drove ashore near Boscastle. Signals of distress were fired, but heavy seas prevented any assistance from the shore, and during the night the vessel became a total wreck. The exact number on board was not known."

David: V: Newport to Stettin. C: Railway track. W: Crackington Haven.... total loss.

Knysna: V: Westport to Bristol. C: Oats. W: Crackington Haven.... total loss.

1849

Three Sisters: W: near Tintagel Head.... total loss.

1850

Principe Alberto: V: Glasgow to Havana. C: Various. W: near Crackington Haven....

"Blown ashore in a heavy gale from the north west, she took the ground soon after midday in the parish of St. Gennys. Carrying a valuable cargo of manufactured bale goods her Spanish crew was saved by the Boscastle Coastguards using Dennett's rocket apparatus...."

1852

Ernesto: V: Venezuela to Hamburg. C: Tobacco. W: Boscastle....

"The wreck of this vessel was found by accident with her bottom just visible at low water... About 60 bundles of leaf tobacco, some canvas and some furniture was saved, also part of a German and a Spanish ensign were picked up. Some letters also came ashore which proved the identity of the vessel. Four bodies were picked up near the wreck, the hull of which had been carried by the sea into a large cavern in the cliff, which had caused her masts to break off."

Caractacus: V: Llanelli to Plymouth. W: Boscastle....

"Having sailed from Llanelli, this vessel was not heard of again, and her wreckage which was washed ashore near Bude was the only clue to her fate."

1857

Britannia: V: Mumbles to St Ives. C: Coal. W: Boscastle....

"On the arrival of the colliers from Wales during the past week, it was found that the Britannia was not among their number, and as she had sailed from Mumbles on Sunday

morning and was seen by the crew of the Alert, of Penzance, to have bore up when off Boscastle on the Monday following, and from that time nothing further has been heard of her, it is supposed that she has foundered with all her crew, including a little boy belonging to Penzance."

1858

Mayflower: V: Llanelli to Teignmouth. C: Culm. W: near Boscastle.... total loss.

Lord Nelson: V: Neath to Teignmouth. W: near Boscastle....
"Foundered; loss on the vessel estimated at £390."

1859

Happy Return: V: Appledore to Cardiff. C: Ballast. W: near Boscastle.... foundered.

Nugget: V: Newport to Troon. C: Railway track. W: Crackington Haven.... complete wreck; cargo was recovered.

Pet: V: Newport to Boscastle. C: Coal. W: Crackington.... total loss.

Trio: V: Truro to Pembrey. C: Copper ore. W: Boscastle....
"John Dennis, a farmer living in the parish of St Gennys was summoned by the police for wrongfully carrying away from a wreck a piece of rope. The defendant was attempting to assist in saving property belonging to the Trio of Truro, wrecked during the late gales. The police, suspecting he had something more about him than he ought to have, stopped and charged him with having wreck in his possession; he denied having any on him, but on being searched, a piece of rope measuring 34ft. was coiled about his body under his coat. He pleaded guilty and was fined double the value of the rope."

1865

Ceres: V: Padstow to Hayle. C: Roofing slate.. W: Boscastle....
"Broke from her moorings during a hurricane, and ran up on the beach where she became a total wreck."

Eugenie: V: Swansea to Barcelona. C: Coal.. W: Crackington....
"Developed a serious leak beyond control by the pump, the captain ran her onshore in a "frightful sea". The crew saved themselves in their own boat; the vessel broke up."

1871

Gitana: W: Crackington Haven....
"Previously a fishing cutter, sold as a pleasure yacht that week, she drove from her mooring in rough weather and became a total wreck."

1872

Unity: V: St Ives to Boscastle. C: Salt. W: Boscastle.... total loss.

1873

Clothilde: V: Nante to Gloucester. C: Barley. W: Crackington....
"Her crew were saved by another vessel."

1877

Adolphe Marie: V: Swansea to Nante. C: Coal. W: Boscastle....
"Drove ashore, and all her crew drowned."

1879

Bottreaux Castle: V: Newport to Boscastle. C: Coal. W: Boscastle....
"Whilst entering the harbour during a S gale, drifted onto the rocks and became a total wreck. Neither vessel nor cargo were insured. The crew were all saved but the ship broke up so quickly they had no time to save their belongings... the ship's boy got his leg jammed and suffered a fracture having to be brought ashore in the hobble boat."

The **Pet** was built at Boscastle by Thomas Avery. She was supposedly named by an old sailor named "Daddy Tregellas" who remarked that her figurehead reminded him of his late wife whom he called "Pet". Tregellas was later offered her captainship. Returning home on the 26th of October 1859 on a voyage from Newport carrying coal, she sank in mountainous seas within sight of the harbour. All on board were lost including Captain Tregellas.

The **Thomasine & Mary** was one of only half a dozen boats to originate from Boscastle. Built in 1855 by Thomas Avery, she was originally a 51 ton smack but was later rigged as a ketch. During her life she was registered in Padstow, Swansea and Bridgewater. On the 7th of September 1926 she was wrecked near Portishead as she journeyed to Hayle carrying barley.

1881
Felix Et Rosalie: V: Tourville to Swansea. C: Ballast. W: near Tintagel....
"Vessel foundered; the crew landed near Tintagel Castle, where they were found by J. Brown of Bossiney, who was out looking for sheep on the cliffs."

1882
Wesleyana: C: Slate. W: Tintagel.... total loss.

1884
Alliance: V: Cardiff to St. Nazaire. C: Coal. W: Boscastle....
"From wreckage washed ashore, it was feared she went down that night in a gale with all her crew."

1885
Resolution: W: Boscastle harbour.... total wreck.

1886
Sarah Anderson: V: Coquimbo to Fleetwood. C: Manganese; dye. W: Boscastle, Trebarwith....
"Owing to tremendous seas, the lifeboat was unable to get near her and it was presumed that she went down with all hands."

1888
Resolution: W: Boscastle....
"Hull much damaged when large pieces of stone fell from the cliffs onto her decks."

1891
Londos: V: Cardiff to Poole C: Fuel. W: Beeny Beach....
"Carrying a cargo of petroleum and benzoline in casks, 100 of which were stowed on deck.. a fire was discovered on board...shortly after midnight in the engine room which spread very quickly and the crew, fearing an explosion took to the

boats and landed at Compass Pt., Bude. After drifting all day the burning steamship went ashore NE of Boscastle watched by hundreds of spectators. Soon after stranding the vessel gave a heavy lurch and what remained of her cargo was thrown into the sea. As each cask hit the water it burst into flames and the sea for a great distance in all directions appeared to be on fire."*

1893
Iota: V: Cardiff to Trinidad. C: Coal. W: Bossiney Cove....
"Having been driven ashore in a gale, nine of her crew were saved by breeches buoy, one of their number having been washed overboard before she went ashore and two others in endeavours to swim to Lye Rock Island." (see photographon the right)

1894
William: V: Swansea to Alicante. C: Coal. W: Crackington....
"On Monday evening at 8pm a mounted messenger reached the Boscastle Coastguard Station with news of a vessel in distress. Six horses were harnessed to the lifesaving apparatus wagon, but when three miles en-route, were advised that the vessel had gone ashore with only one survivor. The sole survivor, mate Svenson stated that his vessel had sprung a leak two days previous and fearing they would sink, the captain decided to run her ashore to save life. Unfortunately, the wind caught her and drove her onto Black Rock at 6pm. Svenson stripped naked and clutching the cook who could not swim, attempted to get him ashore, but lost his grip and let him go, although his body was later pulled from the sea by

someone on the shore. It being dark at the time, no one ashore knew of the wreck until they heard the men shouting for help."*

1896
Thyra: V: Burry Port to Stockholm. C: Coal. W: Crackington.... total loss.

1898
Nina: V: Bridgewater to Truro. C: Bricks. W: Tintagel.... total loss.

1899
Gazelle: V: Llanelli to St. Valery. C: Coal. W: Pentargon.... total loss.
Rosie: V: Fishing vessel. C: Ballast. W: Boscastle.... total loss.

1916
Helena Tregenza: V: Newport to St. Helier. C: Coal. W: Tintagel Head.... total loss.

1917
Rosy Cross: C: Ballast. W: Crackington Haven.... total loss.
William: V: Cardiff to St. Brieuc. C: Coal. W: Crackington....
"The schooner was attacked by a submarine at close quarters, the enemy firing a number of shells into the hull. The crew then abandoned ship, the submariners using their boat to board the schooner and place scuttling charges. The survivors landed at Crackington Haven. The ship's confidential papers and log were destroyed by the master."

1918
Flora: V: Les Sables d'Olonne to Swansea. C: Ballast. W: Tintagel....
"Captured and sunk by German submarine at 3am. Her crew landed safely at Padstow."
Maria Jose: V: Lisbon to Swansea. C: Wine. W: Tintagel Head.... foundered / total loss.

Milly: V: Brest to Barry Roads. C: Ballast. W: Tintagel Head....
"Attacked by a German submarine. The torpedo struck the steamship on the port side...and she sank in five minutes. Two boats were launched, but the men in the after part of the ship soon found themselves in the sea since the stern went down very rapidly. Two men drowned, the remainder being picked up by the S.S. Madame Brooke, and landed at Swansea."

1922

Boy Tom: V: Fishing vessel. C: Ballast. W: Tintagel .... foundered.

1924

Carena: V: Liverpool to Penryn. C: Various. W: Tintagel Head....
"Went missing in a N force 8 gale and was lost with all hands, no trace of the wreck was ever found."

1927

Vervande: V: Cardiff to Las Palmas. C: Coal. W: Tintagel....
"Foundered without trace... five bodies washed ashore... All were Norwegian sailors, four of the bodies were fully dressed, the other nude except for a singlet and socks. Two wore lifebelts with the words "S.S. Vervande-Bergen" on them, and similar lifebelts were washed ashore on the beach. One body...was freely tattooed with a woman's head, flowers and a mast on the right forearm; and a figure of a man in sailor's dress standing by the side of a cross on the other."

1936

Vixen: V: Bude to Boscastle. W: Crackington Haven....
"Following engine failure, this uninsured yacht became a total wreck. Her crew were rescued by the Padstow lifeboat."

1941

Elna E: V: Cardiff to Plymouth. C: Coal. W: Crackington....
"Struck a mine and sank. One crew member lost."

1942

Risoy: V: Southampton to Swansea. C: Iron scrap. W: Tintagel Head.... sank with 450 tons of cargo.

1973

Devron Side: V: Fishing. C: Ballast. W: Rusey Beach....
"Caught fire whilst at sea fishing, crew taken off by helicopter, vessel drifted ashore and was lost."

1991

Mary E: V: Bangor to Isles of Scilly. W: Crackington Haven....
"Drove ashore in heavy weather and went to pieces. Her owner, a 70 year old man, was airlifted to safety suffering from leg injuries and hypothermia. He had attempted to climb to safety but got stuck half way up a 120m high cliff. It seems he did not believe in modern technology, and had no radio or electronic equipment aboard."

1993

Lisa Maria: V: Fishing. C: Ballast. W: near Tintagel....
"Sprang a leak which could not be located, and which soon overwhelmed the pumps. Falmouth Coastguard were alerted who requested another fishing boat to answer the distress call... Towed by this vessel, then joined by the Padstow lifeboat (which despite its powerful emergency pumps was not able to save her), she sank. Her two man crew were both saved."

"The feather of a wren slain on New Years Day, will protect a sailor from drowning by shipwreck."

"A fisherman would never go to sea if on leaving the house he met a priest or a woman."

"White choker is the taboo-name for the clergy."

In St Materiana church, Tintagel lies the body of **Cantanese Domenico**, the 14 year old cabin-boy who perished on the **Iota**. His lonely grave, far from his native home, is marked by a life-buoy bearing the ship's name.

Palaces & Pilchards

The building which now houses the new Boscastle Visitor Centre was converted in 2006, but over the years it has had many previous uses. It was once even a palace - but only for the King of Cornish fish - the Pilchard!

Past Lives

The building has been a restaurant, a cinema named "The Apollo", the village hall, a carpenter's shop, a rope locker and a storehouse for boats and even manure! It was also once the "Wellington Hotel Stables" where horse-drawn carriages were kept and in 1825, it was used temporarily for Methodist services whilst the Chapel in Fore Street was being built.

Its original function however was as a fish processing plant, and it was called "Bridge Fish Cellars". Known to have existed in 1805, it was here that locally caught pilchards were salted, pressed and packed for export.

Boscastle's **Visitor Centre building** complex c.1890

These purpose-built, large rectangular structures with a central courtyard were known as palaces - a rather grand name for a very fishy business!

Bulking the Catch

Once landed, the fresh pilchards would be carried as swiftly as possible from the slipway to the palace.

Here they were gutted by the fishermen, then quickly and skilfully built up into huge, solid, rectangular blocks or bulks on the cellar floor -

The **bulking** process was done mainly by women and children who would work day and night until the whole catch was salted.

each layer of fish separated by a thick layer of salt.

Packing the Hogsheads

After several weeks 'in bulk' the fish were washed and carefully arranged by hand into special wooden "hogshead" barrels.

This task, needing great dexterity and speed, was again usually carried out by the village women. However, itinerant workers also followed the pilchard shoals around the coast of Cornwall finding work when the catches were too large for the local community to cope with.

Each **hogshead** barrel held up to 3000 fish.

The Big Squeeze

In the next stage of the process, the full casks were covered and the lids pressed slowly to extract the fish oil.

Originally this was done using the lever principal, with a large boulder or pressing stone hung from the end of a pressing-pole. The square holes in the cellar walls for the ends of these poles are still visible in the building.

Waste Not - Want Not

Nothing produced by the whole fish curing process was wasted.

Even the smelly blood and brine mixture, which oozed out from the huge bulks, was drained off into tanks and used as a fertilizer.

The oil from the final pressing was a very important by-product and up to 8 or 9 gallons were eventually collected per cask!

Known in Cornwall as "train oil", most pilchard oil was used as lighting fuel and lit the streets of cities as well as homes until the advent of gas and electricity.

Today, the pilchard runs around Cornwall are a thing of the past. However, fishing, although under threat, is still an important part of the Cornish economy employing over 4000 people in the industry. Some £30 million worth of fish are landed in Cornwall each year.

If you've ever wondered what the difference is between a **pilchard** and a **sardine** - here is the answer... Nothing !
They are the same fish - known by the Latin name, **sardina pilchardus** - one is just older than the other, a sardine grows up to become a pilchard.

A **pressing stone**.

A typical **chill lamp**, which used to burn pilchard oil to light the home.

Harvesting the Sea

The earliest written reference to fishing in Boscastle occurs in Launceston's church records and refers to a rather violent event...

"In 1438 there was an unseemly quarrel and blood was shed in the churchyard so that after solemn inquiry the yard was closed as being polluted although a pestilence was raging at the time. The offender was a fisherman from Boscastle and he was punished."

In Boscastle, farming and fishing were once closely linked and many families made their livelihoods from both land and sea, depending on the time of year.

Four main methods of fishing evolved to exploit the ocean's harvest - these were crabbing, long-lining, drifting and seining, each having a distinct 'season'.

Crabbing

Locally, **crab pots** were made from willow shoots (withies) cut from coppiced trees in the Valency Valley.

Crab pots were baited with fish such as gurnard, then lowered to the sea-bed and their position marked by a floating buoy. Each fisherman (crabber) may have owned many pots which had to be hauled aboard and checked every day.

Opposite Boscastle's outer harbour wall is a man-made rock pool once covered by a metal grill. It was used to store live crabs and lobsters.

Long-lining

Baiting long-lines was a long and fiddly task, often involving all the family!

In olden days huge fleets of sailing luggers fished off the Cornish coast using long-lines known as 'boulters' to catch cod, mackerel, ling and pollack.

Long-lining involved setting out a length of hemp line along which up to 700 shorter lengths, or 'snoods' (traditionally made of horse hair), were attached. Each snood carried a hook baited with a limpet, lugworm or piece of mackerel.

Drift-netting

From the 16th to the 19th century, pilchard fishing was a mainstay of the Cornish economy. With their arrival off Cornwall at the end of June, fishermen would sail out to catch the massed shoals using drift-nets.

As the name implies, a row of **drift-nets** were put out at dusk and left to drift overnight like a giant curtain, suspended in the sea by glass buoys or cork pieces. At dawn, the drifting fishing fleet would check their nets for pilchards.

This was hard and difficult work which could take several hours to complete if the catch was large. The heavy drift-nets were hauled in by hand and the entangled fish shaken into the holds. Once back in harbour the fish were scooped out of the boats in wicker baskets (dippers) and taken immediately to the curing yard.

Seining

In the 1800s, at the height of the pilchard fishing industry, seining was the most widespread method of catching this very lucrative commodity. However, by the 1850s seining was in decline as the shoals diminished and by the 1920s seine-netting for pilchards was history.

From July onwards the pilchard shoals came nearer the shore and **seine-netting** began.

The Seine Fleet

Each seine fleet usually consisted of three boats.

The large "sean-boat", would have a crew of 6 or 8 rowers with a helmsman. It carried the seine net (often a quarter of a mile long and up to 60 feet deep).

Two other boats usually belonged to the seine fleet. These were a **voillier** (follower) with a smaller stop or tuck net and the **lurker**, which carried the master and two crew.

Hevva! Hevva! Hevva!

When shoals of fish were sighted a **huer** would raise the alarm by shouting "**Hevva!**" He would then guide the fishermen out to the fish by a system of semaphore signals, originally made using two furze bushes.

The yearly arrival of the pilchards, although expected, was not consistent.

To make sure that the valuable hauls were not missed, lookouts called huers were stationed on the cliff-tops.

Rowing in Rhythm

As the fishermen rowed their heavy boats through the waves the crews would often sing to help them keep time.

Bringing in the Catch

"The cry is up, 'All up!'
Let us all haste away!
And like hearty good fellows
We'll row through the bay.
Haul away, my young men!
Pull away, my old blades!
For the county gives bounty
For the pilchard trades."

A verse of a traditional fisherman's song.

The fishermen would circle around the pilchards and pay out the seine-net to envelop them. The open end would be closed and the whole mass slowly pulled towards the boat, until the fish were trapped.

The catch was then scooped out with wicker baskets (dippers) into smaller boats.

Beefy - Caring for the Nets

A fisherman's **nets** were very valuable possessions and needed constant care and maintenance.

After each trip fishermen's nets were hung out to dry and then "beefied" - checked for damage, mended and soaked in a solution to preserve them. This "barking" liquid usually consisted of oak bark and catechu (a resin-like extract from tropical plants).

How to Cure a Fish

To preserve fish, either for later use or for export, a number of methods were devised for 'curing' them. These included smoking, pickling in brine, dry-salting and by 1873, canning in oil.

In the 1800s, most salt-cured and pressed Cornish pilchards were exported to Mediterranean countries, with Spain and Italy being the main consumers. In 1877 alone, 30 million cured pilchards were exported from Cornwall to Italy.

Fairmaids of Cornwall

"Fairmaids", is a Cornish term sometimes used for preserved pilchards and is thought to be a corruption of the Portuguese "fumado", a smoked herring.

Pilchards destined for export to hot countries like the West Indies would be pressed as usual and then smoked.

There were at least two **smoke-houses** in Boscastle's Quaytown area.

Harvest Highs & Lows

As in all natural harvests there were good and bad years in the pilchard fishing industry. Poor catches meant great hardship and hunger for many - but in bountiful times, fortunes could be made.

In 1834, **30 million fish** were recorded caught off St Ives in a single hour!

In another instance, 120 million were landed in a season, needing 20,000 tons of salt to cure them!

However, unregulated fishing on such a colossal scale inevitably led to the disappearance of large pilchard shoals off the Cornish coast.

Bottreaux Castle

What's in a Name ?

Boscastle gets its name from Bottreaux Castle, the baronial residence of the ancient family of Bottreaux. They came originally from Brittany and settled here after the Norman Conquest.

The original name of the village was **Talkarn**, meaning "brow of a rocky outcrop" in the Cornish language.

In Medieval records the name is spelt in many ways including, Castello Boterel, Botrescastell and even Butters Castell!

The first use of the modern spelling, Boscastle, was in 1550.

Lords of the Manor

The title of Lord of the Manor was passed down through generations of the Bottreaux family.

Over the centuries various branches of the family altered the original **coat of arms**, some adding three toads (c.1100s) or three silver horseshoes (c.1230s) and finally a fearsome griffin (c.1330).

William de Boterell

William de Boterell, Boscastle's first Lord of the Manor, is known to have lived in Wiltshire in 1107 and to have settled here c.1130.

The red and gold chequers forming the background of his coat of arms represented the Earls of Brittany from whom he was descended.

The Castle

After the Norman Conquest of 1066 many French barons were given British lands as a reward for their part in the invasion.

It is likely that the first castle was erected here c.1130 by William de Boterell and was probably a typical Norman construction. This consisted of a motte - a man-made hill, topped with a wooden tower, and a bailey - an area where people and animals could live in relative safety, ringed by a fence and a defensive ditch.

This structure, which must have dominated the village, may have resembled **Restormel Castle** at Lostwithiel.

An idea of what the **castle** may have looked like in the Middle Ages.

Later generations improved the castle by replacing the wooden structures with stone walls to protect and enclose the dwelling rooms and reinforce the strong, circular keep.

The building was also said to have had large dungeons, where both sexes were imprisoned.

Decline & Fall

The castle remained in the hands of the Bottreaux family for over three centuries.

William X Lord Bottreaux, the last male of the family, was killed at the battle of St. Albans in 1461 and left an only daughter, Mary. She was esteemed at that time to be the richest heiress to have ever lived in England and is said to have possessed 100 manors.

In the 16th century the castle was sadly in decline and not a shadow of its former self.

By the mid 19th century all the castle's stonework had vanished. No doubt much of it was reused and incorporated into various village buildings, including pieces of dressed granite, built into the steps of the nearby War Memorial.

In 1873, historian Sir John Maclean wrote…

"On the lower, or northern side, the sites of the outer and of the inner walls are very distinguishable. They were of a circular form and are marked by mounds of rubbish, from which, we are informed, ashlar stones have from time to time been removed for building purposes. The defence on this side must have been strong, but what protection existed on the other sides it is not easy now to discern…"

The famous chronicler **Leland** wrote of it in 1538…
"a Thing…. of smaul reputation, as it is now far onworthe the name of a Castel. The People ther caulle it the Courte."

To reach the **castle site**, walk up the hill past the Wellington Hotel, along Dunn Street, then into Fore Street. The path leading to the castle mound is found beside the War Memorial.

The Castle Site

Today no castle ruins exist above ground but stone footings have been found under the house which sits on top of the great motte.

No Butts...

The stream to the east of the castle site is known as the Butts River and the adjoining fields are also called Butts.

It is thought that this name may originate from the Middle Ages, when compulsory archery practice was imposed on all young men. The mound behind the target is known as a butt.

The French Connection

The spur of land above the village, on which the castle once stood, is known as Jordans and the stream that runs below it on the western boundary is called the River Jordan.

These names are thought to be a corruption of the French - "jardin" (meaning garden) and may refer to the site of the original castle garden.

Among the plants introduced to Britain by the Normans were **carnations** and wallflowers.

The Lost Bells of Bottreaux

According to local legend, a long, long time ago, when Boscastle was known as Bottreaux Castle and a Lord presided over the community, it was decided that the village church was to have a peal of bells that would rival those of all the neighbouring parishes.

So the legend goes...

Three fine bells were cast in London and then sent to the village by sea. After an uneventful journey, the ship with its valued cargo arrived safely off Boscastle's harbour entrance.

The pilot at the helm, a pious Tintagel man, on hearing the sound of his own parish bells drifting over the water duly thanked God for the safe voyage. However the captain of the vessel overheard him and scornfully cried...

"Thank God on land; but at sea thank the captain and his good ship."

No sooner had he said this than a great storm arose and dashed the ship against the rocks of Blackapit. The blasphemous captain perished with his crew and the cargo sank to the sea bed, but the pilot lived to tell the tale.

The bells, so they say, still lie in the bay and sometimes, when a gale approaches, their soulful tolling may be heard from deep beneath the waves...

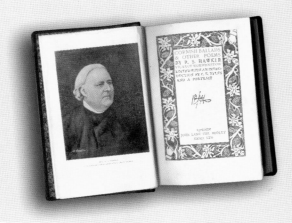

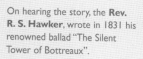

On hearing the story, the **Rev. R. S. Hawker**, wrote in 1831 his renowned ballad "The Silent Tower of Bottreaux".

The Rev. Robert Stephen Hawker (1803–1875)

In 1825, **Robert Hawker** and a fellow student visited Boscastle, staying at the Ship Inn which then stood in Valency Row.

Here, in the early hours, they crept out of the inn and released all the pigs from the village pigsties. They then stole back to their beds to await the resulting outcry and chaos!!

He was born in Plymouth and educated at Pembroke College, Oxford. In 1823, whilst still an undergraduate, he married his godmother who was twice his age. He took Anglican orders in 1831, becoming vicar of Morwenstow in 1834 where he stayed until his death.

In 1843, he introduced the Harvest Festival, the thanksgiving service which is now a major event in the Christian calendar.

He penned the now famous "Song of the Western Men" adopted as Cornwall's unofficial anthem with its stirring chorus of *"And shall Trelawney Die?"*

His tiny hut built of driftwood on Morwenstow cliffs can still be seen and is now the smallest property owned by the National Trust. It was here that he wrote much of his poetry and, as an escape from the ailments of age, smoked opium.

Parson Hawker had a reputation for eccentric behaviour, which has sometimes overshadowed his lifetime of devotion.

He is said to have dressed up and posed as a mermaid on a rock in Bude Bay. For several moonlit nights he entertained growing crowds of curious locals with his wailing before finally plunging into the waves after a rendition of "God Save the King".

He loved bright colours and dressed in a claret-coloured coat, blue fisherman's jersey, a pink brimless hat and a poncho made from a yellow horse blanket - the only black things he wore were his socks.

He kept a huge pig as a pet, along with two deer, named Robin Hood and Maid Marion and nine cats that attended his church services (one of whom he excommunicated for catching a mouse on the Sabbath).

At Stratton he once painted the coat of the surgeon's horse like a zebra, then sent a message to the doctor requiring his immediate attendance. The doctor was obliged to saddle his very strange looking steed and gallop off to his appointment, no doubt to the great amusement of any onlookers!

Holy Wells

Some 212 holy wells are listed in Cornwall. Most are associated with Celtic saints and missionaries, but their sanctity is not necessarily of Christian origin.

Many of the superstitions associated with wishing wells originate from Pagan times when offerings were made to the water deity.

"As supernatural virtue and sanctity were attributed to springs of water previous to the introduction of Christianity, the early Christians found it expedient, the more readily to make converts, not to abolish these customs, but walled up the wells ... and dedicated them to saintly patrons. 'The well had before a Spirit; it now had a guardian saint.'"

J. T. Blight 1858

Five Holy Wells are known to have existed within the parishes neighbouring Boscastle.

St Juliot's well

Like many wells in Cornwall, St Juliot's was venerated for its healing waters and was sought by pilgrims with skin diseases. Reputably there were once curiously carved stones here, one representing the Virgin Mary. These were later buried in or near the well.

St Mathiana's well

Situated near Minster church this well is dedicated to a Welsh princess, variously called St Madrun or St Materiana, who settled here c.500AD. Unfortunately this spot was damaged during the devastating floods which hit the area in 2004.

Money was dropped into wells and **divination** was taken from the rising of bubbles. Crooked pins, thorns and rush crosses were likewise thrown into the water - if the cross sank it foretold of disaster within the year.

In the cult of water worship semi-divine maidens called **nymphs**, inhabited wells, springs and streams. It was believed that they were bound to the water and would die if the source ever ran dry.

St Gennys' well

This well is thought to date from the 7th century when a Celtic monk chose the site for his cell and where Christian converts were subsequently baptised.

Historians debate whether **St Genesius** was a real person or a stirring fictional character. He is said to have been a Roman actor who was converted to Christianity whilst performing on stage sometime in the 3rd century. He is the Patron Saint of actors.

Trethevy well

This is a curious well as it seems to bear no dedication despite the nearby Chapel of St Piran. Other saints associated with the vicinity include St Nectan, whose hermitage is nestled in the valley, St Dennis whose chapel is recorded here in 1457 and perhaps also St David, as Trethevy means "David's dwelling" in Cornish.

Trethevy, thought to have been inhabited by Romans, has a number of historic buildings and is an early Christian site.

St Austen's well

Located at Lesnewth, this well was in use until the end of the 19th century - its waters were carried to the nearby church for the purpose of baptism.

In the Cornish language there are two words for "well", both derived from Latin.
A dug well is **peeth** (Welsh - pydew, Breton - puns, Latin - puteus).
A natural spring is **fenten** (Welsh - ffynon, Breton - feunteun, Latin - fontana), as in Penventon near St Juliot church, meaning "source / headspring / fountain head".

Land of the Saints

From the 4th century AD, Celtic Christian missionaries journeyed throughout Cornwall, spreading the Gospel. Known for their love of the natural world, their religious practice was characterized by pilgrimages to sacred locations.

Around Boscastle, many features remain from this "Age of the Saints". These include ancient wells, crosses and churches, many of which have been dedicated to the holy men and women who dwelt here.

Celtic monks and nuns would often build their cell, or 'lan' in a place of solitude, where they would be free to establish their own separate and radical lives of prayer, contemplation and work.

Minster Church

About a mile inland, tucked romantically into a secluded valley, stands the mother church of Boscastle.

There has been a religious foundation on this site since the year 500AD, when St Madrun chose to establish her cell here and evangelize the area.

Today's church was originally built on the site of a **monastic community** in 1150 by William, Lord of Bottreaux Castle. The Norman structure was enlarged in 1507 and in 1871 was further altered by the overzealous Victorian architect, J.P. St Aubyn.

The stream, which still runs close by Minster church, may have been originally used for healing and for penitential prayer. During the floods of 2004 these waters caused much damage to the church and churchyard resulting in repair works that cost £180,000.

St Madrun

The saint, also known as Materiana, is said to have been born c.440AD the daughter of King Vortimer and the granddaughter of Vortigern (the Brythonic tyrant who is traditionally said to have invited the Anglo-Saxons to settle in Britain).

She married Prince Ynyr, a descendant of the Roman Emperor Magnus Maximus, and together they ruled the Kingdom of Gwent after her father's death. She is then reported to have fled as a refugee to North Wales and in later years to have settled here at Minster with her son, St. Ceidio.

St Madrun was buried where the chancel of the present-day church now stands and *"extraordinary miracles are said to have been wrought at her grave"*.

Forrabury Church

The peal mentioned in the **Bells of Bottreaux legend** are said to have been destined for the tower of this church. Another bell connected with Forrabury is the Holy Handbell of **St Symphorian** which is said to have found its way to Brittany in the 13th century. Only two such rare and treasured items have been recorded as coming from Cornwall.

The church commands a prominent position high on the bare hill overlooking the Atlantic. The tower, rebuilt in 1750, has long been a landmark.

It is dedicated to St Symphorian, a little known saint who came from Autun in Burgundy and who was martyred in 178AD. He was perhaps familiar to the Bottreaux family who built the Norman church here.

Little of the Norman church remains as in 1867 the building was almost entirely rebuilt for the sum of £320.

St Juliot Church

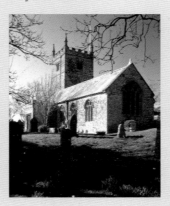

This is perhaps the most famous church in the locality because of its connection with the author **Thomas Hardy** who, as a young architect, came to undertake its restoration in 1872. A memorial on the north wall commemorates this association.

The isolated church of St Juliot overlooks the upper reaches of the Valency Valley and its scattered farms. This has been a place of worship for over a millennium.

The churchyard's shape and site on a spur, suggests that it may have been constructed within an ancient "round" - an Iron Age fort or settlement. The antiquity of the place is apparent from the ancient stone cross that greets you on the right of the gate.

St Julitta

The church is dedicated to a Christian widow from Caesarea in modern Turkey. She was the mother of Saint Cyriacus of Iconium and was tortured and martyred during the persecutions of Diocletian c.304AD.

Some scholars claim that she is fictitious.

Lesnewth's St Michael & All Angels Church

The first church on this sheltered site was built by the Saxons but was ransacked by marauding Vikings.

During Norman times a cruciform building, said to have been of great interest, was erected and a tower was added in the 15th century which has survived to this day.

The current building is the result of drastic restorations in 1862 at the hands of the notorious J.P. St Aubyn who used dynamite as a demolition aid!

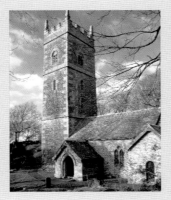

In the great **flood** of 2004 the small stream by the church became a roaring torrent which undermined the churchyard and swept away the footbridge. Thankfully no damage was done to the headstones and an ancient stone cross.

St Michael

Six churches and numerous chapels in the county bear this dedication to St Michael the Archangel, the most famous of which is St Michael's Mount, near Penzance.

It was there in 495AD that a fisherman is said to have witnessed the Archangel Michael miraculously walking upon the waters of the Bay.

The Mount quickly became an important sacred site that would continue to draw pilgrims for over 1500 years.

St Michael the Archangel is the Protector and a Patron Saint of Cornwall.

Look out for the Four Church Walk Guide
This varied walk provides a wonderful opportunity to discover the area's beautiful churches. All are well worth a visit, not only for their setting and history but also because they reveal much about the locality.

Ancient Stone Crosses

"...the Celtic churches were very small, mere oratories, that could not possibly contain a moderate congregation. The saints took their station at a cross, and preached thence."

Sabine Baring-Gould 1899

The majority of these monoliths, found all over Cornwall, were erected between the 8th and the 13th centuries.
They were set up by the side of paths marking the route to a place of religious importance or to show the boundary limits of the parish.

The examples pictured here can be found in and around Boscastle.

Stone crosses were still erected in Cornwall in 1447 to mark burial paths to the church *"for penitents to weep at and processions to stop at"* and where travellers could *"rest and say a prayer to remind them of our temporary stay on this earth."*

Trevalga cross
This is situated beside the path that leads to Trevalga church. It was moved to its present position in 1868 and is believed to date from the 8th century.

Forrabury cross
This stands by Forrabury's church path. It is thought to have been removed from a nearby field called 'Cross Park'. The three noticeable holes in the shaft are evidence of its past use as a gatepost.

Lesnewth cross
This stands in the churchyard of Lesnewth church. It was once used as a pig trough as the reverse of the head bears witness. The cross was rescued and moved here in 1872 and re-erected with a new shaft.

Tregrylls cross
Situated beside the old church path in woods a mile or so away from Lesnewth church. This fine Latin cross was discovered in use as a gatepost in 1988 and moved to its existing site in 1991.

Styles of stone crosses

Inscribed: there are 20 to be found in the county, the majority of which bear Latin inscriptions.

Latin: these are roughly hewn stones with short limbs forming the shape of a cross.

Round / Wheel Headed: there are many types of these crosses but all have circular shaped heads.

Holed: these all display holes piercing the stone forming a rudimentary cross.

Lantern: there are only five complete crosses of this type to be found in the county. They usually display a carved crucifixion scene and figures of the Virgin and Child.

St Juliot churchyard contains three ancient granite crosses...

Tregatheral cross
This cross was found with its head buried in the ground in use as a gatepost at an old mill nearby. It was brought here in 1953 and now stands to the east of the church.

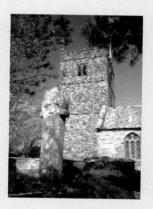

St Juliot's cross
This stands in its original position by the southern stile leading to the Valency Valley.

Anderton Mill cross
Found at the north entrance of the churchyard, this cross was once used as a gatepost in the valley below and was moved here in 1852.

Ancient Trevalga

A stroll through Trevalga churchyard will reveal many graves bearing the inscription "**Boney**", a local family name, pronounced "bunny". Some believe that the ancestors of **William Bonney**, alias **Billy the Kid**, the notorious American outlaw, may have originated from this parish.

Nestling on the seaward side of the Boscastle to Tintagel road is a remarkable "time capsule". The hamlet of Trevalga is unusual in that it is partly managed by a Trust set up by the last Lord of the Manor who purchased it in 1934 for £14,000.

On his death in 1959, provisions were willed to ensure that the estate be kept as a whole and in character, thus preserving a small part of Cornwall for the future.

Whilst most of the church dates from the 13th and 15th centuries there is still some evidence of its Norman origins including the font and north transept arch.

Clusters of slate-roofed cottages huddle along the narrow track leading to the ancient parish church, dedicated to **St Petroc**.

Despite the parish's small population in the 19th century (numbering less than 200 in its heyday), Trevalga's community must have been a pious one as it not only supported St Petroc's church, but an United Methodist chapel and a Bible Christian fellowship.

The Manor of Trevalga

The Manor of Trevalga is one of the most ancient in Cornwall.

The name is believed to derive from the Cornish, Trev-Algar, meaning Algar's Town. Algar was a Saxon nobleman of considerable power and wealth who held Bristol in 980AD.

Feudal dues paid to the current **Duke of Cornwall**, Prince Charles, in 1973.

Mentioned in the Domesday Book of 1086, the settlement was taxed as Melledham and consisted of 120 acres with 4 villagers, 7 small-holders, 5 cattle, 100 sheep and 5 goats.

As with the other Manors in Cornwall, Trevalga owes its allegiance to the Duke of Cornwall. On the occasion of a new Duke, representatives attend a Court at the Gate of Launceston to pay feudal dues - in Trevalga's case, one pair of white gloves.

The Chapel of St James the Apostle

A chapel dedicated to St James the Apostle once stood on the site of the present village hall in Gunpool Lane. During Medieval times this chapel was one of a line of religious houses dotted along a pilgrim route that led to the shrine of St James at Compostela, in Spain.

The pilgrimage to the shrine of St James, was established in the 9th century and by the Middle Ages a line of churches were dedicated to the saint at Kilkhampton, Jacobstow and St Breward possibly marking a route through north Cornwall.

Here at Boscastle stood the Chapel of St James. Measuring around 60ft long by 22ft wide it consisted of chancel, nave and a tower standing some 17ft square. The chapel's date of origin is unknown, but it is mentioned in records dating from 1374 and is thought to have originally been the private place of worship for the Lords of Bottreaux Castle. On the 18th September 1400 however, it was granted a licence for the celebration of Divine Offices and was therefore used for congregational purposes.

By 1744 the chapel lay in ruins but in 1800 its fortunes changed. The building was re-roofed and its tower furnished with a bell which on one joyous occasion was rung with such gusto that it cracked and had to be taken down! The tower remained in use as late as 1837, its bell rung to announce services at Forrabury and Minster.

By 1864, the chapel had been demolished and according to the Rev. A.G. L'Estrange *"its fair corner stones and adornments may be traced in the walls of the adjoining cottages."*

According to tradition **St James the Apostle** journeyed to Spain in 40AD to spread the gospel. Four years later he was martyred in Jerusalem, but his bones were brought back and laid to rest on the site of the present day Cathedral of Santiago de Compostela.

The **ruinous chapel** in 1846. It is said to have been partly demolished so that a boat built inside it could be launched!

Parts of the chapel can be seen in the present village hall. Kerb-stones in Fore Street and the **granite arch** over the old water trough in Gunpool Lane (left c. 1890) are also thought to be from the chapel.

Mystery Stone Bowl

During the immense task of clearing up in the days following the 2004 Boscastle flood a mysterious stone bowl was discovered amongst the debris in the car park.

Where it came from, its age and its use raised much speculation.

It has been suggested that this vessel may be an ancient Norman font as it is similar to ones found at Trethevy Well and Tintagel church.

However, on measuring the relic and studying its features it may be noted that there is a remarkable resemblance to an old corn measure found near Boscastle's castle grounds. There are even blocked holes on either side suggesting that handles or hooks may have been attached at one time.

Could this cast a different light on its origin?

The following extract was written by Sir John Maclean in his "History of the Deanery of Trigg Minor" in 1873...

This **corn measure** was moved to its present position, situated next to the War Memorial near the castle grounds, in the early 1960s.

"By the side of the road leading from Barn Park to Forrabury Church is a stone vessel now used as a water trough, very closely resembling the old stone corn measure now in the Market House at Bodmin. It has the same kind of opening and lip at the bottom, though not the hooks which are on the Bodmin measure. It is between 21 and 22 inches in diameter and twelve inches deep, and in capacity will contain 16 gallons or two Winchester bushels, which at this time is a local bushel.

There is a tradition that it was used as a measure in the Castle whence it was brought, but it is more probable that it formed the standard measure in the Market House."

A **bushel** is the standard measure for dry goods such as flour, wheat, barley, oats, potatoes and fruit. It is thought to have been introduced to England by the Normans with documentary evidence of its use dating back to the 1300s. The **Winchester bushel** was introduced in the reign of Henry VII (1457-1509) and is one of the earliest English measures still in existence. In an act of 1696 it was finally codified as 2150.42 cubic inches. The Winchester bushel was specifically abolished in Britain in 1835 but is still in general use in the USA and Canada.

The Architect

Weymouth,
11th February, 1870.
Dear Sir:
Can you go into Cornwall for
me, to take a plan and
particulars of a church I am
about to rebuild there? It must
be done early next week, and I
should be glad to see you on
the Monday morning.
Yours truly,
G. R. Crickmay

This is the letter that brought Thomas Hardy to Boscastle, where unbeknown to him, his life and the course of English literature would be changed.

In 1870 Hardy was working for an architectural practice in his home county of Dorset and was in charge of church restoration. He was 29 years old, an aspiring, but as yet unpublished author, with a novel entitled "Desperate Remedies" almost complete.

The isolated Church of St Juliot which overlooks the upper reaches of the Valency Valley, was in a perilous state after suffering many years of neglect like many of the churches in the area.

Thomas Hardy 1870

When Hardy first walked into the churchyard on Tuesday the 8th of March it was an austere grey day and a funeral was taking place. Nevertheless Hardy stayed all day, drawing and measuring the ruinous building.

The rebuilding of St Juliot Church commenced in August 1870 and was completed in the spring of 1872.

"The carved bench-ends rotted more and more, the ivy hung gaily from the roof-timbers and the birds and bats had a good time up there unmolested; no one seemed to care."
From Emma Hardy's "Some Recollections".

The tower, the nave and the chancel were all demolished - only the south porch with its fine Norman castellated roof remained untouched.

Hardy later regretted destroying so much of the structure, but in fairness, his work is more sympathetic than the efforts of some contemporary architects.

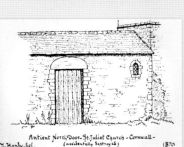

Antient North Door-St.Juliot Church - Cornwall -
T.Hardy.del.   (accidentally destroyed)   1870

This **sketch by Hardy** depicts a Saxon north door that was later accidentally destroyed along with a Medieval chancel screen which he had instructed to be carefully repaired. The carpenter proudly explained... *"I said to myself, I won't stand on a pound or two while I'm about it, and I'll give 'em a new screen instead of that patched up old thing."*

A Cornish Romance

Portraits of **Thomas Hardy** and **Emma Gifford** in 1870.

It was shortly after dark on Monday, the 7th of March 1870, that Thomas Hardy arrived at St Juliot's Rectory after an arduous twelve hour journey from Dorset. He was *"received by young lady in brown"* who introduced herself as Emma Lavinia Gifford.

Emma (standing) her sister Helen & the Rev. Caddell Holder at the Rectory, August 1870.

The Rev. Caddell Holder, rector of the parish, had invited Thomas to stay with them at St Juliot, but being bedridden with gout, the task of entertaining the young architect fell to Emma. During the following few days, as they toured the area, the couple fell deeply in love.

Their courtship was acted out amongst the rugged Cornish landscape and this happy period made a lasting impression on Hardy, influencing his later work as poet and author.

Today the **Old Rectory** is a guest house and its charming interior has a pervasive air of history. Hardy's own guest room, Emma's bedroom overlooking the garden, the parlour where they sang and played chess and the conservatory are all in a remarkable state of preservation.

St Juliot's Old Rectory dates from 1847 and has remained virtually unchanged since Hardy first set eyes on the place in the spring of 1870.

The times spent within these walls affected him deeply and are remembered in numerous poems such as "At the Piano", "The Frozen Greenhouse" and "The Sundial On A Wet Day".

The Author

Emma encouraged Thomas from the start to pursue his literary talents, giving him the confidence to choose writing over his career in architecture.

In the autumn of 1872, Hardy's first published novel, "A Pair of Blue Eyes" was serialised in Tinsley's magazine. Throughout his life-time this remained his personal favourite.

The story is set in his imaginary county of "Wessex", but many scenes can be traced to the landscape around Boscastle and the disguised place-names are recognisably local: Castle Boterel is Boscastle; Dundagel is Tintagel and Endelstow Rectory is St Juliot's Rectory.

At the close of 1872, Hardy published "Far From the Madding Crowd" and its success promoted him to the forefront of the literary world. With an income assured, Hardy and Emma decided to wed and they were married in September 1874 at St Peter's, Paddington. The couple never returned to Cornwall.

The cliff scene from **"A Pair of Blue Eyes"** illustrated by W. J. Morgan.

Despite the fame and fortune that followed his success as an author, Hardy's marriage was not a happy one.

In old age Thomas and Emma lived very separate lives; he often visiting London for long periods and she retiring to an attic room in their Dorchester home.

The difference in Thomas and Emma's characters created an unbearable tension between them added to by their childlessness. Emma felt that she had married beneath her social position, whilst Thomas on the other hand felt he had married his intellectual inferior.

Then, suddenly in the autumn of 1912, Emma died. Hardy filled up with remorse and grief, shocked by how much her death affected him.

Emma Hardy in the summer of 1911.

Thomas Hardy aged 73 in 1913.

The Poet

Delving amongst the possessions of his newly deceased wife Emma, he found her recollections of their carefree courtship in Boscastle all those years ago.

In a desperate attempt to regain those feelings he travelled back to Cornwall to revisit the places where they had been happy together. This journey resulted in an outpouring of 21 of his most emotional poems, published as "Poems of 1912-13".

The dramatic landscape of North Cornwall and his early visits to Boscastle made an indelible impression on Hardy.

Beeny Cliff in particular seemed to have had a hold on him and here he returned some 43 years later. His feelings and memories were expounded in the poems "Beeny Cliff", "The Figure In The Scene", "It Never Looks Like Summer" and "Why Did I Sketch".

Hardy's **sketch of Emma** at Beeny Cliff on a wet Monday in August 1870.

Hardy's **memorial tablet** to Emma in St Juliot's Church.

Hardy's last visit to Cornwall was in September 1916, when he came to inspect a stone memorial in St Juliot Church, which he had designed for his late wife.

Following the trip he wrote "The Famous Tragedy of the Queen of Cornwall", it was his final homage to Emma in the guise of the Cornish Queen Iseult.

In all, Hardy wrote more than one hundred poems about Emma.

On the 19th of August 1870, Thomas and Emma enjoyed a **picnic** of fruit and wine on the banks of the Valency River. Here they lost a glass tumbler and the day was recalled fondly by Hardy. Not only did he sketch the event but wrote touchingly of this episode in two poems, "Under the Waterfall" and "Best Times".

Geological Origins

In the vastness of geological time, the area we now know as Boscastle has seen immense changes and transformations. It has been elevated from seabed to mountain top, contorted by tremendous pressures and then eroded into the complex and dramatic landscape we see today.

Thick beds of sediments were washed down into deep waters that existed here 360 million years ago. Heavier grains such as sand settled first, then silt and finally muds. These layers, called "turbidites", may have been laid down in a matter of hours.

Here, some 300 million years ago, 80 million years of compacted sediments were folded, overturned and baked into the dramatic, contorted rocks that are seen in the cliffs of this coastline. Some of the folding was so extreme that the rock beds were turned over, producing a zig-zag pattern known as "chevron folds".

The spectacular topography of "over-deepened valleys" such as at Pentargon are a product of the Ice Age when huge volumes of meltwater swept down gullies during thawing periods. Another dramatic feature here is the 120ft waterfall flowing over the cliff edge.

360 million years ago...
Boscastle and the upper part of north Cornwall is submerged under the waters of a vast delta which lies just above the Equator. During this period masses of sediments are washed down from jungles and swamps where Wales currently lies and the area rapidly silts up.

310 million years ago...
Collisions between the earth's major land masses have now squeezed the ocean bed upwards and gradually Boscastle emerges from the waters.

300 million years ago...
As the tectonic plates continue to shunt into each other, a wave of deformation sweeps through the area, dramatically altering the bedrock. This vast upheaval results in the formation of a mountain range, likened to the present day Himalayas.

250 million years ago...
Tectonic activity in the area has drawn to an end and the mountains are now collapsing under their own weight, causing faults in the process. Erosion by wind, water and ice continues to shape the landscape.

240 million years ago...
North Cornwall is now in the middle of a desert-like phase which lasts a staggering 80 million years.

Shaping the Landscape

200 million years ago...

The climate has now changed, becoming wetter with rising sea levels and increasing instances of flooding.

150 million years ago...

Cornwall is now an island experiencing a warm, humid climate similar to present day Jamaica. It is a landscape of gently rolling hills and swamps inhabited by dinosaurs.

100 million years ago...

Boscastle lies beneath the rising seas once more and only the granite stumps of the high ground around what is now Bodmin Moor are exposed.

2 million years ago...

The area is now enveloped by the Ice Age and is dominated by permafrost, like that experienced in parts of Canada today. Ice bergs float offshore and Cornwall is joined to mainland Europe.

11,500 years ago...

The Ice Age ends and the geological period we are now living in begins. The elements continue to erode and on the coast the sea exploits weak points in the rock, such as fault lines and mineral veins, forming caves and causing cliff falls. As sea levels rise Cornwall is once again slowly sinking beneath the waves.

Etched into the surroundings of Boscastle is the evidence of man's endeavours to exploit the environment, harvest its bounty and alter it to his own advantage. A struggle that has gone on for at least 4000 years.

Man's Early Impact on the Landscape

As early as 3700BC man had started to shape the land. Forest clearances had begun making way for farming and a more static lifestyle. This led to the building of hill forts, tumuli and ancient field systems.

Evidence of the area's pre-historic origins includes settlements such as the one found on Willapark headland just south of Boscastle harbour.

The name **Willapark** comes from the Cornish words **whylas** and **parc**, meaning enclosed lookout.

The **Stitches** on Forrabury Common are thought to date back to the Celtic Dark Ages. Here 40 strips of land without dividing hedges are still cultivated on a four year rotation. It is one of the few remaining examples of this method of farming left in the country.

Field boundaries often reflect the underlying geology - here a local hedge is made of **quartz** and **slate**.

Development of the Field System

Fields of all shapes and sizes are an integral part of the rural scenery around Boscastle. They illustrate the evolution of agricultural practices from the Celtic open field system through to the later Medieval era (c.1400 - 1700) when narrow plots were enclosed. The Agricultural Revolution and Enclosure Acts of the 18th and 19th centuries brought further changes and large, more uniformly shaped, hedge-bound fields became the norm.

Most hedges in Cornwall, even the tall, grassy-banked ones that line many of the rural roads, have the hidden skeleton of a carefully crafted stone wall.

Local Building Materials

The older buildings in Boscastle show both the versatility of local materials and the resourceful skills of bygone craftsmen. Good quality slate made durable roofing material whilst poorer quality stone was ideal for walling.

Unseasoned (green) oak harvested from local woods was extensively used for roof timbers. Drying out slowly over the years they sometimes contorted resulting in the dramatic roof-lines now synonymous with the village. Some of these timbers have been dated to the 16th century.

Recycling

The Cornish have always been natural and keen recyclers of useful materials. Timbers from wrecked ships were given a new lease of life as roof-beams and suitable ballast from visiting ships was sometimes used as stonework. Even the ruins of Bottreaux Castle itself were spirited away over the years to be incorporated into newer buildings.

This characteristic herringbone pattern, known locally as "**Kersey Wave**", attractively demonstrates the skills of the traditional hedger.

Distorted **rooflines** are indicative of old buildings, whose beams and rafters were usually of green oak.

Old masonry built into the village hall in Gunpool Lane and kerb stones in Fore Street are recycled remnants of the ancient **Chapel of St James**.

The predominant rocks found around Boscastle are:

Slate - originally laid down as fine mud some 410-290 million years ago.

Sandstone - formed from consolidated grains of sand sediments deposited between 360-290 million years ago.

Dolerite - a volcanic rock that forms many of the area's headlands, dating from 385-365 million years ago.

Farming Practices

Until the end of the 19th century most families living in the village would have been self-sufficient to some degree, having a productive kitchen garden and a pigsty. It was common practice for half the pig's carcass to be traded for enough salt to cure the other half.

Harvesting **early potatoes** - a traditional and local speciality. In the 19th century Boscastle potatoes were renowned as they were the earliest to crop in Britain

Traditional Agriculture

Farming around Boscastle is traditionally mixed, creating a typical mosaic of arable fields, pasture, hedgerows, woodland and scrub. The old methods of pastoral management and rotational cropping still continue today.

Scything of scrubland was once a common sight - furze (gorse) and bracken were both harvested for fuel and animal bedding.

Some farming traditions have long since disappeared but others, such as clearing cliff top scrubland, have been re-introduced. In some areas the cliffs have become overgrown with moribund heather, bracken and gorse. To combat this cattle, sheep and even goats have been brought back as part of managing cliff top vegetation. The National Trust, in particular, have maintained or reintroduced this grazing management in order to benefit nature conservation.

These practices, have recreated the crucial habitat for a successful re-introduction of the large blue butterfly.

The **large blue butterfly**, formerly widespread on the coastal valley slopes of north Cornwall, became extinct here in 1975 (and in the rest of the UK in 1979), due to the scarcity of its short turf habitat.

Clifftop grazing can be beneficial by controlling invasive species. This is done to best effect when the flowering season is over allowing the spread of annual plants.

Quarries

Perhaps one of the greatest impacts on the Boscastle landscape over the last 200 years has been the extent of quarrying in the area.

Large portions of cliff were blasted away and the remains of these workings are still visible today - silent reminders of a bygone industrial age.

Slate

At one time, almost everything in the Cornish home was made of slate as it was cheap, durable and readily available... walls, roofs, flooring, fireplaces, shelves, sills, water tanks and even the kitchen sink!

At nearby Buckator Quarry the quality of the stone was such, that large faultless slabs were cut for billiard tables.

Slate was quarried in vast amounts from the cliffs along this stretch of coast from the 14th century until the onset of World War II.

Once prepared or "dressed", the slates were transported by mule and cart to loading points where small coasters awaited below. Techniques were perfected for bringing boats into shallow waters close to the cliffs or beaching them at safe havens such as Tintagel. Slate was then taken by sea to many locations along the Bristol Channel, around Land's End to the English Channel ports and even to the Continent.

Cliff quarrying was a dangerous business and operated throughout the year in all weather conditions. Quarrymen would attach themselves to the cliff with lengths of rope (left, c. 1930), swinging out of the way as blocks of slate came free.

The waste produced by this industry was enormous, some 75% of all quarried slate was tipped back over the cliff.

Slate quarries are still active in the area, including the world famous Delabole Quarry, which has supplied slate for well over 600 years.

The **finger dump** at California Quarry on the Boscastle cliffs is a good surviving example of the wastage involved in cliff quarrying.

Mines

During the 18th and 19th centuries an explosion of mineral mining occurred in Cornwall making the county a world centre of innovation and technological development.

Mines opened at an unprecedented rate and the Boscastle area did not escape its own share of prospecting, though most local mines were uneconomic and had a relatively short lifespan.

Manganese

Quantities of manganese are known to have been produced in the area and an ore-crushing mill operated in the village during the 1850s. However most manganese shipped from here, came from mines in the Launceston district. The ore was exported to Liverpool and Glasgow where it was used in the glass industry.

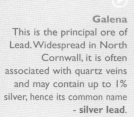

Pink rhodonite
This specimen contains dark **manganese** oxides. "Manganese brown" as it was sometimes known, was used as a dye to colour wool and cotton.

Silver lead

This is also known to have been mined in the vicinity. A mine on the cliffs of nearby Trevalga, by the name of "Great Well Town Lead & Silver Mine" was operational in 1837. Further work was carried out at Grower Rock in 1845 where adits driven in at the foot of the cliff are said to have had wooden gates.

Galena
This is the principal ore of Lead. Widespread in North Cornwall, it is often associated with quartz veins and may contain up to 1% silver, hence its common name - **silver lead**.

Iron ore

Boscastle was also an important exporter of the district's minerals including vast quantities of iron ore brought from the Launceston area, in particular from Trebursye Mine. In 1862, amongst great publicity, a traction engine journeyed to the port. It drew two iron trucks containing 14 tons of ore and returned with 9 tons of coal. Thereafter it regularly made three trips a week to Boscastle carrying as much as 20 tons of ore.

Boscastle harbour was once used to export **iron ore** which was also imported in great quantities with some 130 tons shipped here in 1870.

Minerals of the Area

Although only manganese and silver lead were commercially mined in the vicinity, many other minerals are found here including the following...

Arsenic
This highly poisonous metal, is obtained from **arsenopyrite**, also known as **mispickel**. Arsenic was in great demand as a herbicide and insecticide from 1860 onwards and between 1870-1902 Cornwall was producing 4,000-8,000 tons annually, about half of the world's output.

Antimony
This mineral was of great strategic value in the 18th and 19th centuries as it was used in the casting of cannon shot. Today it is used in pewter, electrical batteries, fireworks, matches and dyes.

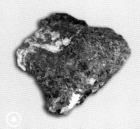

Cassiterite - Tin
Cornwall was once the largest tin producer in the world, an industry that dated back as far as 1750BC when Cornwall traded with Mediterranean civilisations. Today China, Indonesia, South America and Australia are the main tin exporters.

Chalcopyrite
This is the principal ore of **Copper**, the oldest metal known to mankind - mined 5000 years before gold was found!
Cornwall once led world copper production, peaking in 1855-6, when over 200,000 tons of ore were mined.

Dolomite
This is a common mineral that can be found in massive beds of sedimentary rock, sometimes several hundred feet thick. It is used in the manufacture of some cements and also as a source of **Magnesium**.

Fluorite
Originally referred to as **fluorspar** by miners, it is the most popular collectors mineral in the world, after quartz. It is used as a flux in steel and aluminium processing and is also the source of fluorinated water and toothpaste.

Minerals & Rocks

Iron Pyrite
This is the classic **Fool's Gold**. Although common and containing a high percentage of iron, it has never been used as a significant source of iron. It has been mined for its sulphur content though, and during WWII it was used in the production of sulphuric acid.

Jamesonite
This is one of a few sulphide minerals that form fine hair-like crystals and has been called **feather ore** and **grey antimony**.

Quartz
The most common mineral on the face of the Earth. One of the notable properties of quartz is its hardness - harder than a steel file. Large boulders of this mineral can be found dotted around Boscastle and are particularly impressive seen built into the old harbour wall which dates back to 1584.

Dolerite
An igneous (volcanic) rock, also known as **blue elvan** and **greenstone**, which is rich in iron, potassium, magnesium and aluminium. There is a considerable variety of this rock to be found in North Cornwall, but generally, all are distinctivly hard and thus form many of the prominent headlands around the coast e.g. Willapark, Stepper Point and Pentire.

Shale
Often veined with quartz, this rock consist of consolidated mud sediments whose grain size are finer than sandstones. These grains were deposited in very slow moving water such as river deltas and date from the Carboniferous period.

Tuff
Pronounced "toof" the name comes from the Latin, meaning "porous stone". The rock consists of the cemented loose product of a volcanic eruption and is grouped according to its parent lava (e.g. **basalt tuff**, **andesite tuff**), as well as its grain size - the finest being **dust tuff**.

The Atlantic Shore

The shores around Boscastle provide a haven for a wide variety of flora and fauna adapted to live in habitats dominated by the sea and salt-laden winds.

Inaccessible coves and towering rock faces offer seclusion for grey seals and sea birds, whilst the cliff-tops support a host of plant and insect species.

A stroll along the coastal footpath - only minutes from the busy village centre - provides a chance to witness some very special wildlife. Here are a few interesting examples...

Seals

The aptly named Seal Caves that pepper the cliffs to the north of Boscastle, are the haunt of grey atlantic seals. Here, their mournful songs can be heard and they can be glimpsed basking on the rocks.

"... the sillie people of Bouscastle and Bossiney do catch in the summer seas divers young soleys (seals), which, doubtful if they be fish or flesh, conynge housewives will nevertheless roast, and do make thereof very savoury meat."

Although now a protected species, grey seals were once caught in the caves below Beeny Cliff and eaten by the local inhabitants.

Puffins

The sea parrot, as it is sometimes known, was once a common sight along the shores of Boscastle. In the past, colonies on nearby islands supported thousands of nesting birds.

Today there are possibly only a dozen pairs of **puffins** nesting in the area.

Sadly there has been a massive decline in numbers due to factors such as oil pollution, overfishing and predation by gulls and rats.

Fulmars

These petrels, related to the albatross, fly with stiff wings, riding the updraughts of the steep sided cliffs.

Formerly a northern species, they were once rare visitors to Cornwall, their first recorded brood being in 1944.

Fulmars defend their nests by spitting out a foul smelling oil a distance of up to two metres.

Stonechats

These robin sized birds, have a distinctively sharp call resembling two pebbles being tapped together.

They are often seen perched on the uppermost spikes of gorse bushes, in which it nests - hence the local name of furze chat.

Although common here in Cornwall, the **stonechat** is faring less well on the Continent where it is endangered.

Peregrines

These falcons are the fastest moving bird in the world reaching speeds of around 300 km/h (185 mph) when plummeting after prey. They have been popular as a falconers bird for centuries and were once protected by royal decree, reserving them for the use of kings.

Today, trained **peregrines** are used at many military airbases to clear runways of other birds.

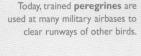

Thrift

Thrift, or sea-pink as it is commonly known, thrives in every type of seashore location.

The compact green cushions clump together, often forming vast springy drifts and are in leaf throughout the year. However the plant is most spectacular when it flowers between May and July.

The pink, papery flowers of **thrift** are noted for attracting wildlife and have been a favourite garden edging plant as far back as the 16th century.

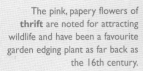

Furze

Furze is the local name for gorse, the spiky-leaved bush so typical of this coast. Its thick, spiny leaves reduce the amount of moisture loss and its tough, pliant stems put up with the most exposed and windy of locations.

The two local species both have coconut scented, yellow flowers,

Gorse seeds were once used as a pesticide against fleas and the woody stems were cut for kindling.

which bloom at slightly different times, giving rise to the saying... *"When gorse is in blossom, kissing's in season."*

57

Heathers

Both ling and bell heathers are found in abundance around the coastal slopes of Boscastle. These shrubs have had many traditional uses ranging from fuel, animal feed, bedding and thatching material.

The flowering stems of **heathers** are still used to produce orange dyes.

Thyme

This small, prostrate, wiry plant forms cushions on the cliffs of North Cornwall and during warm, sunny days from June to August diffuses a fragrant, aromatic perfume.

Thyme is the host plant for the larvae of the rare and endangered large blue butterfly. The eggs are laid in the buds of thyme, the seeds of which the larvae will eventually feed on during July and August. After about three weeks the larvae drop to the ground where, remarkably, they are found by red ants who carry them back to their nests. Here the larvae feed on ant grubs then hibernate over winter and after pupating, emerge as adult butterflies sometime in June.

Thyme has long been used as a medicinal herb to treat chest problems such as coughs and bronchitis.

Butterflies

This part of the coast is a wonderful place for butterflies. Over 20 species have been recorded here, including the dark green fritillary.

Fritillaries are fast and powerful flyers well able to cope with strong sea winds.

How Green Is My Valley

The name **Valency** is thought to come from the Cornish "**melyn-jy**" meaning mill house.

The Valency Valley, with its river and wooded slopes, supports a vast array of wildlife.

Today this seemingly 'natural' habitat cloaks a past where trees were regularly harvested and the stream was once employed to power several waterwheels and mills.

Valency Woods

Throughout history these woods have provided a living for many, supplying raw materials for numerous traditional uses.

Trees were cut here for fuel and carpentry. Bark was collected for tanning leather, withies harvested to make crab pots, baskets and hurdles, whilst the woods were also a source of food and medicinal herbs for the local inhabitants.

Trees in the Valency Valley were traditionally **coppiced**, a practice of cutting trees close to ground level, in order to produce a self-renewing crop of wood. This provided timber for many purposes, including charcoal-making.

Amongst the myriad of tree species found here are...

Willow

There are many species of this deciduous, fast growing tree. They were traditionally pollarded every 4-5 years to produce a crop of straight poles. The shoots and leaves were fed to animals.

Ash

A large deciduous tree that grows quickly and can live up to 200 years. Its tough and elastic timber is highly prized by carpenters. It is also valued as fuel, burning well even when green.

Hazel

A deciduous shrub and small tree frequently coppiced and used for fencing. The hazel's forked twigs are still used for divining water and other treasures.

Beech

This large, deciduous tree matures at 120 years old and may grow to 140 feet high with a trunk of 21 feet in girth. One of its chief uses was in the making of charcoal for the manufacture of gunpowder.

Holly

This evergreen tree tolerates shaded positions and was pollarded in former times and used for winter animal feed. Its berries are poisonous. At Christmas holly was used locally as a Christmas tree.

Oak Trees

The oak for many centuries was the chief woodland tree of Britain and the Valency Valley is considered to be a remnant of the original tree cover of these isles.

Two species of oak exist in the valley, sessile and English. Both are deciduous. Growing slowly they can reach the great age of 1000 years.

Trees were often coppiced in the past on a long rotation of perhaps 50 years. The bark being rich in tannin, was used for tanning leather.

Acorns

The two species of native oaks can be distinguished by the acorns they bear.

Those of the **English oak** occur often in pairs on long stalks.

The acorns of the **sessile oak** are stalkless.

Purple hairstreaks

These butterflies live in colonies and fly in summer around the tops of oak trees where they feed mainly on honey dew - a sweet liquid secreted by aphids.

The botanical name of the **oak - Quercus -** is said to be derived from the Celtic quer (fine) and cuez (tree).

* * *

The name **druid** stems from the Celtic words for oak and for knowledge.

The Tree Canopy

Oak trees, along with other native broadleaves, provide shelter and food for numerous creatures.

Below the tree canopy, insects, birds and mammals feed and hunt amongst the shrubs that flourish in the dappled shade.

Tawny Owls

These are Britain's most common owls. Their large eyes and sensitive hearing makes them successful nocturnal hunters, whilst by day they often roost in tree hollows.

Jays

These colourful members of the crow family play an important role in the life of an oak wood by collecting acorns which they bury to retrieve and eat at a later date. Some of these nuts are forgotten and germinate into saplings.

Speckled Wood

This butterfly favours forest clearings where it likes to sunbathe. It usually has two broods, flying April to June and again from July to September.

Pearl-bordered Fritillary

This sun-loving butterfly of woodland glades is found from May to June and lays its eggs on violets.

Badgers

These rarely seen mammals emerge from their burrows (setts) after dusk to forage. They are omnivorous, eating insects, worms, fruit, roots, birds eggs and small rodents. Setts are well maintained and if left undisturbed may be used for hundreds of years.

Roe Deer

These shy animals are the smallest of our native deer species. The dense woodland undergrowth offers good cover for adults who browse at dawn and dusk on grass, leaves, berries and young shoots. When alarmed they bark, much like a dog.

Spring Time Flora

A walk through the Valency Valley in spring, when the trees are still in bud, is perhaps the best time to see the early flowering woodland plants.

Hart's-tongue Fern
Like most ferns, this thrives in damp and shady conditions. It is easily recognised by its shiny, spear-shaped leaves. In country districts, an ointment was made of its fronds for burns, scalds and piles.

Ramsons
Other names for this familiar, strong-smelling woodland resident are Londoner's lilies, wild garlic and stinking nanny. Young leaves, surprisingly mild in taste, may be eaten in salads, soups etc.

Bluebells
This much loved bulb can be found in a variety of shades including pink, purple and white. Its sticky juice was once used as a bookbinders' gum and to set feathers onto arrow shafts.

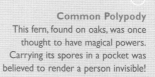

Wood-anemone
This graceful plant, also known as moggie-nightgown, appears from March to May. It spreads at the rate of only six feet every 100 years, so finding it in quantity is a sign of ancient woodland.

Common Polypody
This fern, found on oaks, was once thought to have magical powers. Carrying its spores in a pocket was believed to render a person invisible!

In Man's Company

Boscastle is a village surrounded by a variety of wildlife habitats, many of which are in fact man made.

From ancient meadows to road-side hedges, old quarries, graveyards and farms - adaptable plants and animals have colonised them all.

Even a short stroll through the village will reveal both commonly sighted and unusual plants, insects, birds and animals. Whilst the centuries old hedgerows, of which there are 30,000 miles in Cornwall, sustain a vast microcosm of wildlife.

Violets

The delicate blooms of these well-loved plants are an early springtime treat along lanes and footpaths.

Of the many **viola** species the dog violet, which has scentless flowers and the sweet violet (named from its sweet scent) are most commonly found here.

Violets are the food plant of the rare fritillary butterflies which occur in the Boscastle area.

Lords-and-Ladies

These curious looking **lilies** commonly found under shady hedges have, over the centuries, been given a variety of names including cuckoo pint, snake's meat and willy lily!

In the past, their poisonous roots were baked and ground as a food thickener, called Portland Sago. It was also used as clothes starch, but often blistered the launderers' hands.

A drop of **Lords-and-Ladies'** poisonous juice will cause a burning sensation in the mouth and throat for hours.

Snowdrops

When Thomas Hardy first visited St Juliot in March 1870, the **churchyard** was filled with snowdrops.

The delicate white blooms have long been associated with purity and were grown in religious sites throughout Britain.

The **snowdrop** is not a native plant but was introduced to Britain from Italy in the 17th century.

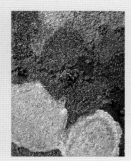

Stonecrops
These succulents, form dense cushions which in June and July are a mass of short-lived starlike blossom. Two species can be found here, the **biting stonecrop** which has yellow flowers and more commonly the **white stonecrop**, which bears white and pink blooms.

Lichens
These are a combination of two organisms, **fungus** and **algae**, living intimately together. This was first observed by the author Beatrix Potter. They absorb nutrients from the air and can indicate an unpolluted environment.

Hoverflies
Commonly seen hovering over flowers during early summer and autumn, the adults feed solely on nectar and pollen whilst their larvae eat aphids. **Hoverflies** become darker in colder weather so that they can warm up more efficiently.

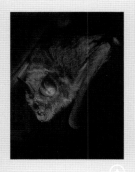

Greater Horseshoe Bats
One of **10 bat species** to be found in Cornwall, it has a wingspan of up to 40cm and is the largest of its type in Europe. They are mostly active around woodland edges and roost in caves, adits or old buildings.

Slow-worms
These **legless lizards** are usually found hiding under sun-warmed stones and are are known for their longevity, up to 20 years or more in the wild. They eat slugs and snails and give birth to live young.

Barn Owls
These beautiful birds are most active at dusk, silently hunting for rodents. Voles are their staple diet, with an adult bird consuming approximately three per day. **Barn owls** have exceptional hearing and can catch prey in total darkness.

River Valency

Since the **2004 flood** the Valency Valley has been studied closely and has revealed historical flood evidence on a major scale.

It has recently been designated as a County Geology Site (formerly known as RIGS).

This tumbling river supports a host of aquatic life such as insect larvae and small fish like sticklebacks. These in turn attract many birds including...

Grey Wagtails

The underparts of this elegant little bird are a **striking lemon-yellow**. It can be seen perched on river rocks, pumping its long tail up and down. When walking, its movements are quick and jerky, but once airborne its flight is undulating with long glides between wing beats.

Dippers

As its name suggests, this bird can often be seen plunging into the water where it hunts for **aquatic insects** and **crustaceans**. Dippers sometimes take over grey wagtail nests. There are records of them helping to feed grey wagtail nestlings.

Valency views by Thomas Hardy

On his visits to Boscastle, Thomas Hardy often walked through the Valency Valley and the landscape made a lasting impression on the young author. Not only did he sketch the scenery, but he also wrote touchingly of it in two poems, "Best Times" and "Under the Waterfall".

The Boscastle Flood
16th August 2004

At midday on the 16th August 2004 the remnants of Hurricane Alex, which had crossed the Atlantic, converged along the high ground around Boscastle. Great cumulonimbus clouds, 12,192m (40,000ft) high, formed causing a succession of thunderstorms. The prevailing winds kept these stationary for many hours.

This, along with the topography of the area, was the key to the catastrophe that became a landmark in British history and made headlines throughout the world.

Some Facts & Figures

■ At its peak, nearly 300mm fell in an hour - that's 5mm a minute.

■ The flood peaked between 5:00pm and 6:00pm when 632,000 litres (139,000 gallons) of rainwater fell every second.

■ All in all it has been estimated that over 2 million tonnes (440 million gallons) of water swept through Boscastle that day.

■ Localised torrential showers began at Camelford and at the top of Boscastle at around 12:00pm on the 16th of August 2004 and persisted for 5 hours.

■ The River Valency began to breach its banks at around 3:30pm and at 4:00pm a 3 metre wall of water surged through the village at an estimated speed of 40mph.

■ The first firefighters from Delabole Station arrived at 4:15pm.

■ 29 out of the 31 Cornwall County Fire Brigade stations were involved in the incident. They remained at Boscastle for 7 days after the flood, assisting in the clean-up operation.

■ RAF rescue helicopters were scrambled at 4:22pm. Eventually 7 helicopters arrived at the scene, airlifting 100 people (including 6 firefighters) to safety.

■ Around 1,000 residents and visitors are believed to have been affected by this devastating event. They witnessed the largest peace time rescue in the history of mainland Britain.

■ 58 properties were flooded, 4 of which were demolished: the Visitor Centre, Clovelly Clothing, Things and the Harbour Lights.

■ A further 40 properties were flooded in Canworthy Water, Bude, Helebridge and Crackington Haven - with severe flooding at Otterham, Week St Mary, Marshgate, Millook and Camelford.

■ Four footbridges along the Valency Valley were washed away as were many others in neighbouring valleys.

■ 84 wrecked cars were recovered from Boscastle's harbour and streets, a further 32 could still be out at sea.

■ The flood caused £50 million worth of damage.

■ Miraculously there were no fatalities and only one reported injury.

3.30pm

4.00pm

4.30pm

5.00pm

These dramatic sequence of images were taken by Pam Durrant.

The Flood & its Aftermath

Aerial photograph of Boscastle taken during the flood of August 16th, 2004

Photo supplied by www.apexnewspix.com   Tel: 01392 824024

The Car Park

Some 130 cars were parked in the car park when the flood hit. Over 80% of these were washed through the village and into the harbour, some out to sea.

The Original Boscastle Visitor Centre

This was opened in 1994 and was a popular attraction. Some one million people had called by the summer of 2004. Situated in the car park, it bore the brunt of the flood as a 3m (10ft) wall of water swept down the valley. It was from the small remaining roof space of the building that 12 people were airlifted to safety whilst the structure was literally dissolving into the deluge below them.

Amazingly one of the **internal displays** was washed ashore at Barry, South Wales - with some of its geological rock samples still attached! The Visitor Centre building was eventually demolished and its slate floor relocated to outside the entrance of the new Visitor Centre.

Swollen waters of the Jordan River rose 10 feet inside the **Wellington Hotel** destroying much of its historic interior.

The Jordan River

This river, which flows into the Valency, devastated the dwellings lining its banks, inundating them with boulders and mud from the valley above.

Debris washed down the **Valency Valley** eventually piled up against the bridge and formed a dam. Water then backed up and flooded the nearby properties.

The retail property known as **Clovelly Clothing** collapsed like a pack of cards when vehicles carried by the torrent collided with its old walls.

Valency Row

This became a scene of devastation as the flood diverted into the narrow street, depositing vehicles, tree trunks and other debris along the way.

The New Visitor Centre

This building, then housing a shop and restaurant, suffered considerable internal damage, the waters reaching almost to the ceiling and washing all the flooring away.

Bridge

Built in 1887, the lower bridge became an obstacle to the raging waters, acting like a dam. However it withstood the onslaught and only lost its parapets. The nearby Harbour Lights shop with its centuries old, undulating roof-line, was completely demolished by several vehicles battering into its walls. The Youth Hostel next door also suffered extensive damage with its foundations seriously undermined.

The Harbour

This was the final resting place for some of the 116 cars which had battered their way through the village. Several metres of thick mud and debris smothered the haven within which lay countless belongings of those present on the 16th August 2004.

Freak or Frequent?

The flood of August 16th 2004 is known as the worst natural disaster to have hit the village and among the most extreme ever experienced in Britain. However, this severe weather event was just not a freak of nature, as flash floods in summer affect localities throughout the British Isles almost annually. The 1950s saw nine extreme rainfall events, the worst being the Lynmouth disaster of August 16th 1952.

Extreme Floods in Cornwall

16th July 1847 - Boscastle and North Cornwall.
This devastating flood swept down from Davidstow Moor, washing away all but two of the bridges along the River Camel - Wadebridge and Helland were the only structures to survive.

4th August 1938 - the South West.

6th September 1950 - Boscastle, Camelford and Bude.
The remarkable feature of this flood was the torrential rain, the heaviest in living memory, and the rapidity with which the Valency River rose and burst its banks. Trees 6m (20ft) high were ripped up along the valley and carried along the river. They passed through the road bridge but then piled up against the lower bridge forming a dam that caused the waters to back up into the village.

16th August 1952 - Lynmouth (Devon).
The flood sadly claimed 34 lives and left 420 people homeless. 93 houses and 28 bridges were destroyed and 38 cars swept out to sea.

28th October 1827 - Boscastle.

"One of the most awful days I ever experienced at Boscastle. It rained very heavily in the morning & whilst we were in the Chapel increasingly so - when about to leave the whole street was filled with a body of water rolling down & carrying all materials with it - that devastation & ruin were its concomitants - by about 1 o'clock the rain ceased leaving the fine McAdamised road in complete ruin from Polrunny to Dunn Street. At Bridge teams of Wagon Horses were saved with difficulty. Pigs also belonging to the Cottagers were taken out of ye Roofs of Houses. Mr Langford & Cottagers the West side of the Bridge suffered much. But thro the goodness of God on the East River [Valency] the waters were raised but little & our property preserved in safety - I would mark the finger of Divine providence & acknowledge his loving kindness."

From the Journal of Thomas Pope Rosevear.

8th June 1957 - Boscastle and Camelford.
203mm of rain fell in 24 hours, 140mm of it in 2½ hours with hail drifts over ½m (2ft) deep.

3rd June 1958 - Boscastle.
The Valency River is estimated to have risen 4½m (15ft) above its normal level in the short space of 20 minutes after a cloudburst above the village. This tragically claimed the life of 45 year old Mr Berryman, the Bandmaster of Boscastle Silver Band, who was helping neighbours. He was washed off his feet and swept down the river into the harbour where he drowned.

Boscastle suffered a **flood** in 1963 as snow on the high-ground thawed and flowed down into the valley's rivers.

6th February 1963 - Boscastle.
Many villages and towns in north Cornwall suffered flooding during this week as the heavy snows that had hit the country began to thaw.

The **steep-sided valleys** that typify the area act as huge funnels and can produce true flash floods after a sudden cloudburst or prolonged heavy rainfall.

The Brown Willy Effect

The Brown Willy Effect is a meteorological phenomenon that occurs on occasions in north Cornwall.

It is named after the hill Brown Willy, the highest point on Bodmin Moor, where weather fronts tend to converge sometimes resulting in heavy showers. Rainwater filters into the many rivers that spring on this high ground and flow down to the sea.

The South West Coast Path

The South West Coast Path National Trail passes through Areas of Outstanding Natural Beauty, National Parks and many other designated landscapes. It is not just the longest National Trail, it is the 'Jewel in the Crown'.

One sixth of it is in the District of North Cornwall, (111miles / 178km). The stretch between Crackington Haven and Tintagel, although strenuous, will reward your efforts with magnificent scenery.

1 Crackington Haven was once a small harbour. Early in the 19th century, ambitious plans were proposed to build a large port here with a lighthouse, dry dock, a town and a railway. The idea was later abandoned.

2 Cambeak, with its twisted rock formations, is a striking example of coastal erosion actively sculpting the land.

3 There is a good path down to Strangles Beach where, at the northern end, there is a spectacular rock arch known as Northern Door.

4 High Cliff is not only the highest point on the Cornish coast path, but claims to be the most lofty place in England at 732ft (223m). Although bleak and inhospitable on stormy days, it boasts dramatic views all round.

5 Beeny Cliff was once enjoyed by Thomas Hardy - his novel "A Pair of Blue Eyes" features this area. Seals often bask on the rocks below known as the Beeny Sisters.

6 Pentargon inlet has a dramatic 120ft waterfall.

7 From Penally Hill there is an excellent panoramic view of Boscastle harbour.

8 The white tower on top of Willapark was built in 1827 as a summer house; it was later used by the Revenue men and is now a National coast-watch lookout.

9 Short Island provides a breeding ground for birds such as puffins, guillemots and razorbills. Nearby is the curious rock formation known as Ladies Window.

10 The dramatic gorge of Rocky Valley is where the 60s hit song "Sunshine of your Love" was supposedly penned!

11 Bossiney Cove, with its Elephant Rock, is one of the most popular bathing beaches on this part of the coast.

12 The second Willapark headland also bears the remains of an Iron Age cliff castle.

13 Tintagel is most famous for the Arthurian legends. A ruined castle can be seen on the Island and information on this and much more can be gleaned in the Tintagel Visitor Centre.

At approximately 640 miles (1030km) long, the **South West Coast Path** is the longest National Trail - over twice as long as the Pennine Way.

If you walk the entire path you will ascend 91,000 feet - the equivalent of climbing Mount Everest three times!

More than 1 million day visits to the Coast Path are made each summer.

Along the whole path there are over 925 stiles, 240 bridges, and 2764 signs and way-marks.

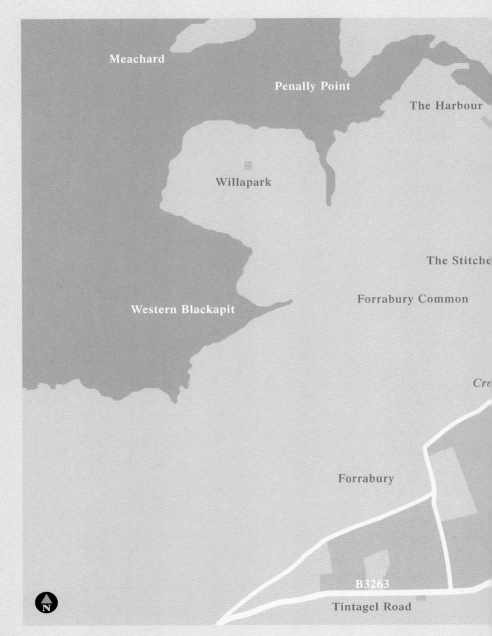

Meachard

Penally Point

The Harbour

Willapark

The Stitche

Western Blackapit

Forrabury Common

Cre

Forrabury

B3263

Tintagel Road

N